FORTY NORFOLK ESSAYS

R. W. KETTON-CREMER

Forty Norfolk Essays

NORWICH 1961

JARROLD & SONS LIMITED

Printed and bound in Great Britain by
Jarrold & Sons Ltd, Norwich

PREFACE

For many years past I have contributed occasional essays on matters of local history to the *Eastern Daily Press*. I have no inclination to reprint most of these. But in some I have used historical material, from public and private archives, that might otherwise have remained unpublished; and in others I have brought people and incidents back from an oblivion that was not wholly deserved. I have made a selection of those essays which I think worthy of preservation; and I now offer them, under the imprint of a Norfolk firm, to the East Anglian audience for which they were originally designed.

I am very grateful to the Editor of the *Eastern Daily Press* for his kindness in allowing me to reprint the essays in this form. My thanks are also due to the authorities of the Bodleian Library for permission to quote extensively from the Tanner Manuscripts, that rich repository of East Anglian material. Certain other debts of gratitude are acknowledged in the text.

Any profits derived from this publication will be given to the Friends of Norwich Cathedral, to assist in their great work of repairing, adorning and maintaining the Mother Church of East Anglia.

R. W. K.-C.

Felbrigg Hall
Norwich
May 1961

To

EDMUND *and* PRISCILLA BACON

with admiration and affection

CONTENTS

THE SEVENTEENTH CENTURY

The Founder's Tomb *Page* 11

The Florists' Feasts 13

Preparations for War 16

Sir John Spelman 19

The Sin of Eating Custard 21

The Winter Rising (I) 24

The Winter Rising (II) 26

The Cathedral in Danger 29

Pounds, Shillings and Pence 31

The Parliament of 1656 34

The Death of Cromwell 36

Parish Affairs 39

Sir Christopher Calthorpe 42

Bishop Sparrow 44

The Troubles of Sir Peter Gleane 46

Repertorium 49

THE EIGHTEENTH CENTURY

The Last of the Blennerhassetts 55

Henry Cross-grove 57

A Norfolk Poll Book   59

The Diary of John Ives   62

The Mission to Cawston   65

Cromer in the Eighteenth Century   67

Revolutionary Norwich   70

THE NINETEENTH CENTURY

Robert Forby   77

The Life of Cotman   79

The Norwich Magazine   81

The Eastern Arboretum   83

SPANNING THE CENTURIES

The Vanished Heydons   89

Baconsthorpe Castle   91

Some Paston Footnotes   93

The Paston Memorials   95

Norfolk and the Law   97

The Green Yard   100

History from the Monuments   102

Salthouse and the Sea   104

Letting Loose the Tap   107

Some Forgotten Painters   109

"Battles Long Ago"   112

Forgotten Controversies   114

Wolterton Hall   116

Index   119

THE
SEVENTEENTH
CENTURY

THE FOUNDER'S TOMB

ONE OF BROWNING'S FINEST POEMS is the monologue in which an Italian bishop of the sixteenth century gives orders on his deathbed about the construction and adornment of his tomb. His last hours are tormented by the fear that his heirs will prove false to their trust, and fob him off with inferior materials and an ungrammatical epitaph instead of the peach-blossom marble, the *lapis lazuli,* the pure green jasper, the bas-relief in bronze, the "choice Latin, picked phrase, Tully's every word" upon which he had fixed his dying thoughts. Such situations must often have arisen; and some rich men preferred to set up their tombs and perfect the Latinity of their epitaphs while they were still alive.

Among these was Sir William Paston, one of the leading figures in Norfolk at the beginning of the seventeenth century. In 1608 his long, prosperous and useful life was drawing to its close after a final act of beneficence, the foundation two years earlier of the Grammar School at North Walsham; and he felt that the time had come to "order his tomb". Wiser than Browning's imagined bishop, he determined to supervise in person every detail of the monument which would bring his semblance before the eyes of posterity. In all matters of business he was in the habit of consulting his trusted friend Sir Thomas Knyvett of Ashwellthorpe, whose daughter Katherine had married his grandson Edmund Paston; and several of his letters to Knyvett have survived and are now in the Bodleian Library at Oxford. Most of them relate to estate and family affairs, the purchase of land or the gift of an "exceedinge fatte Bucke". But they also contain a few references to Sir William's tomb in North Walsham Church, and the original contract for it is preserved in the same volume of papers.

This document has been somewhat damaged and a number of words are missing, but its general purport is clear enough. It was drawn up on 23rd February 1608 between Sir William Paston on the one part, and William Wright, citizen and haberdasher of London, and John Key, citizen and freemason of London, on the other. Wright, although a member of the Haberdashers' Company, was like Key a well-known monumental mason. Sir William was in fact entrusting his monument to extremely competent artists, and their price was accordingly high—the very substantial sum, in the money values of three centuries ago, of £200. The design was to be carried out "accordinge to a platt drawen under the hand of Sir Thomas Knevet of Ashwelthorp in the said countie of Northfolk". (It is made clear later in the contract that Sir Thomas did not actually furnish the design, but was acting as an intermediary with the consent of both parties.) The monument was to be "finished ended carried and set upp in the said parish church of North Walsham in the said county of Northfolk in such place as the said Sir William Paston shall appoynte att or before the second daie of October next ensuing the date herof". I think it is very probable that this was Sir William's birthday, on which he would complete his eightieth year. He certainly had some particular fondness for the first two days in October: the Foundation Deed of his Grammar School had been sealed on 1st October 1606.

The contract lays down the dimensions and materials of every portion of the monument. Its central feature was to be "the picture of a man in Armor restinge upon his Arme of five foote and a halfe longe in Allablaster"; and we are reminded of Browning's bishop once again as we read of the "faire blacke marble stone", the three tall "Parramidies", the "Pillers, Epitates, Writtings and Armes", the painting and the gilding. Everything was provided for: Sir William would pay the carriage of the monument down to Norfolk, but the masons must "fynde themselves meate, drinke, bricke and mortar" while it was being erected. He signed the contract and sealed it with his signet of a fleur de lys, and it was witnessed by Sir Thomas Knyvett and three other Norfolk neighbours.

Wright and Key made good progress with the work, and Sir William sent Knyvett on 26th May the first instalment of the £200 which was due to "my Tombe maker". In the same letter he asked Knyvett "to be in hande with Mr Cobb the carrier for my pickture the which was delivered to him longe sithence: wherein he neyther delt well with me nor you in that he hath kept the same soe longe in his handes . . . me thinketh it remaineth in his warehowse at Bisshopsgate: therefore you shall doe well to rebuke him for the same". I think this "pickture" was probably the effigy of "a man in Armor" intended for the monument, which we have just seen described as a picture in the contract: although it may have been the fine painting of Sir William, venerable in his civilian attire of sober black, now the cherished possession of the school which he founded.

It would seem that the monument was erected at North Walsham within the specified time, and that Sir William was able at the beginning of October to contemplate his own effigy in alabaster, the pyramids and pillars, the richly-painted armorials of all his ancestors, just as we see them today. But one thing remained to be done: his epitaph was not yet inscribed upon the slab prepared for it. We do not know to whom he had entrusted its composition—perhaps it was the work of Michael Tilles, whom he had appointed the first headmaster of the Grammar School. On 14th October he sought once again the advice of Sir Thomas Knyvett. "I have thought yt good", he wrote, "to send you enclosed by my servant this bearer, the Epitaphe made for my Tombe, the which I have good liking of: and therefore if you be of that minde I will have it ingraven upon the stone out of hand, desiring you to return me the same by my messenger if it be to your good liking, that yt may soe goe forward presently, otherwise to sett downe yor minde to the contrary . . . that thereby my Tombe may be perfected according to yor advise and direction". In due course the epitaph was finally approved, and the praises of the old knight's piety and beneficence were inscribed upon the stone above his recumbent effigy. He died just two years later, on 20th October 1610. Three centuries and a half have passed since then: but upon the first day of October in every year a commemorative service is still held in North Walsham Church, and the boys of the Paston Grammar School walk in procession past the stately tomb of their founder.

THE FLORISTS' FEASTS

ALMOST EVERY SEVENTEENTH-CENTURY ACCOUNT of Norwich includes some reference to the beauty of its gardens and the skill of its gardeners. John Evelyn, when conducted round the city by Sir Thomas Browne in 1671, noted that "the suburbs are large, the prospects sweete, with other amenities, not omitting the flower gardens, in which all the inhabitants excel". In the eyes of Thomas Fuller, "Norwich is (as you please) either a City in an Orchard, or an Orchard in a City, so equally are Houses and Trees blended in it, so that the pleasure of the Country, and populousness of the City, meet here together."

Fuller attributed the Norwich cult of flowers to the Dutch immigrants who settled in the city during the sixteenth century. "They brought hither with them, not onely their profitable crafts, but pleasurable curiosities. They were the first who advanced the use and reputation of Flowers in this City." It may well have been so. Certainly a Dutchman was in practice at Norwich as a kind of consultant landscape-gardener as early as 1575. In that year Sir Thomas Kytson summoned "the Duchman gardner" to advise him on the laying out of his garden at Hengrave Hall in Suffolk; and subsequently he paid him forty shillings "for clypping the knotts, altering the alleys, seting the grounde, finding herbs, and bordering the same".

By the sixteen-thirties the annual Florists' Feasts, which are also said to have been introduced by the Dutch, had become a regular feature of Norwich life. These annual functions seem usually to have combined a flower-show and a play. Nothing could be more innocent than a flower-show; but any suggestion of a play was certain to antagonise the Puritan elements in the city and its corporation. In consequence, a good deal of dissension arose over the Florists' Feasts. The Puritans did their best to suppress them; people with a less gloomy outlook on life were eager to defend them.

My attention was lately drawn to an unpublished poem in an Oxford library by William Strode, one of the chaplains of Bishop Corbet, that steadfast adversary of Puritanism and lover of poetry. Strode's poem was a prologue, specially written (and no doubt with the Bishop's approval) for one of the Florists' Feasts. The Feast in question must have taken place between 1632, when the Bishop was appointed to Norwich, and 1635 when he died. Apparently the Puritans (it was typical of their reasoning) had accused the Florists of impiety in celebrating the rites of Flora, a pagan deity. Strode indignantly denied the charge:

> *Our feast we call,*
> *Only from Flowers, from Flora not at all.*

And he went on to expound, in a delightful passage, the point of view held by the reasonable and tolerant churchmen of his day. He conjured up the loveliness of spring, the fragrant air, the singing of the birds, and above all the flowers:

Those joyfull presents which a God hath sent
That loves a cheerefull taker. As they'r meant
For pleasure, so we take them. 'Tis our choyce
Of service, way of thanks, thus to rejoyce,
And prayse him in his gifts, while ev'ry sense
Injoyes his various workes of excellence.

Another clerical supporter of the Florists' Feasts was the Rev. Ralph Knevet, the chaplain of Sir William Paston of Oxnead and the author of a considerable number of poems. He wrote an elaborate pastoral in five acts, *Rhodon and Iris*, for the Florists' Feast of 1631. It was published later in that year, and is now extremely rare. Knevet was not a poet of the quality of Strode, and I doubt if a revival of *Rhodon and Iris* at the Maddermarket Theatre would prove a box-office success. But it is, so far as I know, the only surviving full-length play written expressly for the Norwich stage during the seventeenth century.

It is dedicated to Nicholas Bacon of Gillingham, a gentleman "fervently addicted to a speculation of the vertues and beauties of all flowers". (It was to his son of the same name and the same tastes that Sir Thomas Browne dedicated *The Garden of Cyrus* a quarter of a century later.) Then follows an address to "his much respected friends, the Society of Florists", full of veiled allusions to the Puritan members of the corporation who had shown hostility to their Feasts. There are also commendatory verses by several of Knevet's admirers —Richard Pert, William Dennye, John Mingay, and a certain M. S. who wrote in Latin and compared his friend to Ovid.

The scene of *Rhodon and Iris* is laid in Thessaly. The characters are shepherds and shepherdesses, and almost all of them bear the names of flowers. Rhodon and Iris—the Rose and the Lily—are the hero and heroine. But the lovesick Eglantine is enamoured of Rhodon; and the lands of Rhodon's sister Violetta are invaded by the turbulent Martagon. Some light relief is provided by Clematis, Eglantine's maid and Gladiolus, her page. Two evil intruders, Agnostus the impostor and Poneria the witch, seek to bring discord to peaceful Thessaly by furthering the designs of Eglantine and Martagon. But all is set to rights in the last act by the descent of Flora, brought from her tranquil bowers by "the noyse of these tumultuous broyles"; and the wicked schemers are sentenced to lifelong exile from Thessaly.

Several of the scenes must have had an allegorical significance which was plain enough to the Norwich audience. For example, when one of the characters speaks of "a schismatical selfeconceited Coxcombe in an antient Corporation", and another dresses up as a militia officer although

> *I am altogether ignorant in the words of command,*
> *And know not one posture neither of Musket nor Pike,*

everyone would have known who were aimed at. Such topical satire would have blended well with Knevet's tropes and metaphors on the subject of flowers, while the eye was enchanted by the actors in their floral disguises. *Rhodon and Iris* must have given much harmless pleasure in the city of gardens in that spring of 1631, with the Civil War and the Puritan ascendancy still more than a decade away.

PREPARATIONS FOR WAR

FOR CENTURIES the church of Hevingham has stood beside the highway which leads from Cromer and Aylsham towards Norwich, looking southward across its village to the heathlands which the famous planter Robert Marsham transformed two hundred years ago into flourishing woods. In and around the churchyard stand what must be some of the oldest Spanish chestnuts in the country; and within the church are such features as the remarkable foreign stained glass in one of the nave windows, and the splendid candelabrum which found its way to Hevingham, I do not know when or by what means, from St George's Church at Great Yarmouth. The upper part of the porch formerly contained a chamber or "parvise", of which only the windows and the blocked doorway now remain; and I was interested to discover, in a document among the Tanner manuscripts in the Bodleian Library, that this chamber was regarded by the authorities of South Erpingham as a suitable repository for the "hundred store" of ammunition during the early months of the Civil War.

The rector of Hevingham, the Rev. Edmund Porter, was something of a pluralist. He was a prebendary of Norwich Cathedral, and apparently held another living in Suffolk as well. His Royalist sympathies had already brought him into trouble; in September 1642 he had been sent for in custody by the House of Commons, and eventually he was ejected from all his preferments. It is pleasant to record that he lived to enjoy his own again at the Restoration, and did not die until 1670; but in the early winter of 1642 he was probably still in custody, and certainly in no position to object when the authorities of South Erpingham Hundred, Parliamentarian supporters to a man, crammed the little chamber above his church porch with materials of the most inflammable and explosive kind.

The document to which I refer was a certificate signed by one Thomas Edwards and dated 1st November 1642. It shows that "the vestre over Hevingham Church porch" then contained 6 barrels of gunpowder, each weighing 1 hundredweight, and 12 hundredweight of bullets in their casks. There was also a large quantity of "the best match", and a smaller amount of "fflemish match" which was evidently regarded as an inferior brand. The matchlock, not yet widely displaced by the flintlock, was a cumbersome weapon, and the lengths of smouldering "match", which had to be kept dry at all costs, added greatly to the difficulties of seventeenth-century warfare. In addition the stores included implements for making trenches and emplacements—35 pickaxes, 30 "hodd sholves" (which may have been the same as "hodding-spades", defined by Forby as "a sort of spade principally used in the fens, so shaped as to take up a considerable portion of earth entire"), 30 mattocks, 15 axes and 15 beetles.

All this was for the use of the local militia; and another document in the same volume of papers is a summons from the Deputy Lieutenants to "our very loving friend Sir John Potts, Knight and Baronet, captayne of a company of foote within the hundred of South Erpingham", ordering him to muster his company on Heydon Ollands on 13th November. Sir John Potts lived at Mannington Hall, and was one of the members of Parliament for Norfolk and an ardent upholder of the Puritan cause. We may be sure that his company did him credit at the muster on Heydon Ollands; and he continued to figure prominently in the affairs of the Eastern Association, both political and military, in the years to come.

The Tanner manuscripts also contain lists of the subscriptions, in money or in plate, offered by the supporters of the Parliament at public meetings held in such local centres as Aylsham, Holt and Walsingham. Sir John Potts and Sir John Palgrave, who lived at North Barningham, each volunteered £100, besides "two horses furnished and 10 foote armed". Their less opulent neighbours gave in proportion. The well-to-do rector of Letheringsett subscribed £50, his colleague at Edgefield could only afford £10. A certain Robert Bacon promised £5 "out of my poore weake estate". Roger Bulwer of Guestwick, in an outburst of enthusiasm, undertook to send the whole of his plate, "one hundreth pounds if it weigh soe much". Amongst all these eager Puritans it is curious to find Sir William Paston of Oxnead, who was presently to disclose his Royalist sympathies and to be severely mulcted for them, but who at this stage still retained his Deputy Lieutenancy and his company of militia, and evidently hoped that some accommodation between King and Parliament might yet be reached. He subscribed more generously than anyone else, as befitted the richest man in north Norfolk—£200 and six horses fully furnished.

Sir John Potts chose to pay his contribution, as no doubt did many others, by sacrificing a portion of his plate. A list of what he sent has been preserved—6 silver candlesticks, 2 banqueting dishes, 1 preserving ladle and dish, 8 plates, 1 basin, 1 "Broath Standing Bowle", 1 chafing-dish, 1 vinegar cruet, 1 closet candlestick, 1 porringer, 3 trencher salts. Samuel Butler described in *Hudibras* how the Parliamentarians

> ... *coined bowls and flagons*
> *Int' officers of horse and dragoons;*
> *And into pikes and musqueteers*
> *Stamped beakers, cups and porringers.*

Here we can see the very process; and the same thing was being done by both sides all over England. The art of the goldsmith and silversmith in this country had reached a level that has never since been surpassed, and we can only lament the disappearance of so many beautiful and curious objects into the melting-pot. But it was one of the most important methods of providing those sinews of war which enabled Englishmen to fight against Englishmen during the tragic years to come.

SIR JOHN SPELMAN

THE OPENING MONTHS of the English Civil War were full of uncertainty. The general position was still confused, and all men of moderate views were hoping that a peaceful settlement might yet be reached. In Norfolk the Parliamentarian majority, determined and well organised, was enrolling men, collecting money, melting down plate; but the ordinances for the sequestration of Royalist estates were not yet in force, and individual Royalists gave open expression to their views. The friendly traditions of the English countryside are not easily broken; and many Puritans, however strong their religious and political convictions, were not eager to take action against neighbours with whom they had been associated for years in social intercourse and local administration. Gradually, however, feelings grew angrier; violent quarrels broke out at meetings of magistrates and deputy-lieutenants; the scattered Royalists began to be marked men, their speeches noted, their movements watched with suspicion. Open conflict could not be delayed much longer.

I lately came across an unpublished letter, among the Tanner manuscripts in the Bodleian Library, which vividly recalls this atmosphere of uncertainty and mistrust. Its writer, Sir John Spelman, was the eldest son of the great Norfolk jurist and antiquary Sir Henry Spelman. He was himself a scholar of considerable distinction; like his father, he was deeply versed in the Anglo-Saxon language, and he had written a valuable life of King Alfred. From the outset of the war he took up an openly Royalist attitude. He refused to contribute to the funds of the Parliamentarians, was accused of "affronting" their Committees, and in December 1642 had spoken so warmly in favour of the King's cause at an assembly of the gentry of the county that he "was commanded to depart the meeting". His Puritan neighbours and relations—another John Spelman, his cousin, sat in Parliament for Castle Rising—were not likely to indulge this sort of conduct indefinitely, and in other circumstances he might have left home and joined the King at Oxford; but the King had sent him a letter on 21st January 1643, expressly directing him "not to quit Norfolk or suffer himself to be carried thence, his personal services and residence there being especially needed".

At this time Sir John Spelman was living at Stinton Hall in Sall; and on 2nd February 1643, he addressed a long letter to his neighbour and kinsman Sir John Potts of Mannington. Potts was one of the two members of Parliament for the county: a Puritan of moderate views, but none the less an active supporter of the Parliamentarian cause. No doubt he was keeping a very close watch on the activities of his Royalist neighbour at Sall; but their families were still on visiting terms. Spelman had been away from Sall, and was told, on returning home, that his wife had gone to call on Sir John and Lady Potts at Mannington in company with another neighbour, Mrs Houghton, who lived with her husband at the manor-house of Wolterton. He felt obliged to explain his subsequent movements to Potts in some detail.

"It was my ill fortune coming late last night to my house . . . to be informed that my wife was gonne to waite on you, in Mrs Houghton's coach, and that she went from thence to Woolterton with hir, I easily crediting it because it being past 6 of ye clock, it was I thought too late for hir to venture on horseback in ye darke. I tooke my horse againe and came about to Woolterton, and what by fetching about and missing my waye made it so late that I found Mr Houghton in bedd and much troubled at my so late coming to his house; as for my wife, I found she neither was, nor had been there. I was sorry, that I had exposed my self and my neighbour to be had in jealousy for any thing that such a nightly coming to him might (in these times) insinuate."

How clearly the feeling of those ominous months is reflected here —the suspicion and distrust between neighbours, the anxiety lest a visit late at night should be misinterpreted, the shadow of civil war beginning to darken the ordinary courtesies of country life.

Spelman goes on to justify his own political attitude, and, while not concealing his personal sympathies, to disclaim any intention of fomenting trouble in Norfolk. Here, again, the contemporary atmosphere is vividly reproduced: Spelman is voicing the uncertainties of all reasonable men, whatever their party, in that sad and anxious time. According to Mr Houghton, Sir John Potts had "affirmed that there was a designe and endeavour of some to raise forces and to procure the coming of his Majesty's armey into ye county and to joyne with ye Papists here. Sir, if I were not unjustly and without all candour publiquely defamed for a malignant and Popishly-affected, I should never entertaine any jealousy that I might be meant any share in such charges, but being by that crimination now made capable of partaking of every calumniation in that kinde, I hold it my duty even to Christianity to protest my innocence. . . .

"I am perswaded that the raising force, by either ye one side or ye other, would bring the warre into the county, which (God is my witness) I have to my understanding and power faithfully sought and still shall seeke to divert; and were that endeavour as well pursued on the one side as I perswade myself it has been and yet is on the other, I am confident our county, as it is privileged above all other by scituation, so it would have enjoyed that priviledg in immunity from ye common calamity. In the same judgement hath Mr Houghton ever concurred; and truly, Sir, it was and (I am perswaded) yet is your own judgment also."

The veil of time, lifted for a moment by the survival of this letter, descends once more on Sir John Spelman the moderate Royalist, and Sir John Potts the moderate Puritan, and the anxious Mr Houghton. We do not know whether they met to discuss their perplexities and disagreements, or whether their ladies continued on the same friendly terms. But Sir John Spelman was not to ride much longer about the increasingly hostile Norfolk countryside. A few weeks later the King summoned him to join his army at Oxford; and there, on 25th July of the same year, he died suddenly and in the prime of life of "the Camp Disease", an epidemic which had broken out among the troops in the overcrowded city and its neighbourhood. The King learnt of his death with deep regret, and specially requested Archbishop Ussher to preach his funeral sermon. Sixty years afterwards his life of King Alfred was published at Oxford under the care of Thomas Hearne; and that admirable editor paid tribute to the "Religious, Loyal and Learned Author" whom we have seen losing his way in the muddy Norfolk lanes in the darkness of a February night.

THE SIN OF EATING CUSTARD

IN THE LITTLE CHURCH of Sotterley near Beccles, I lately noticed a ledger-slab commemorating the Rev. Sir Lionel Playters, rector of Sotterley and Uggeshall, who died in 1679. The name seemed familiar; and presently I remembered the account, in Walker's *Sufferings of the Clergy*, of the sufferings of this particular clergyman. When the Civil War began, Playters only held the living of

Uggeshall, and had not yet succeeded to the family baronetcy; but he was a courageous and outspoken man, prominent among those of the Suffolk clergy who held Royalist views, and he soon ran into trouble.

As early as 1642, at the very outbreak of hostilities, his house was raided by a party of troopers, who broke open his stable doors and took away two good horses. When, in Walker's words, "he had the Confidence to demand by what Authority they did it, they reply'd, *Pistol the Parson,* and fired two or more Pistols at him". He would not be intimidated, but openly displayed his Royalist sympathies, denouncing the rebellion from his pulpit, refusing to take the Covenant, and steadfastly maintaining the rites and ceremonies of the Church of England. Like so many of his brethren, he was haled in due course before the committee appointed by the local Parliamentarian leader, the Earl of Manchester. Twelve witnesses appeared against him. One of these accusers reported him as having said that "he had a Parcel of Hemp to sell, and hoped it would bear a good Price; because, if the Times continued, a great many would want Hanging; and, that rather than fail, he would give it to the King to Hang up the Roundheads". From a different source Walker learnt that another chief article against him, and a principal cause of his ejectment, was "his eating Custard after a scandalous manner, of which, it seems, he was a very great Lover".

The custard of the seventeenth century was a rich confection of eggs, cream and sugar; and Mr Playters was said to have heightened its flavour by adding sack, the favourite wine of Sir John Falstaff. In the eyes of the stricter Puritans all kinds of feasting and merriment, and especially the time-honoured enjoyments at Christmas, were wholly sinful. Their disapproval extended to the fare which was traditional on such occasions; and this charge against Mr Playters is a striking corroboration of the famous lines in *Hudibras,* where Butler describes how the Puritans

> *Quarrel with minc'd-pies, and disparage*
> *Their best and dearest friend plumb-porridge;*
> *Fat pig and goose itself oppose,*
> *And blaspheme custard thro' the nose.*

There was much to be said for the Puritan point of view on the major issues of the time. But how detestable one finds their intolerance, their self-righteousness, their hatred of art and pleasure and gaiety—the whole attitude of mind against which Sir Toby Belch had uttered his memorable protest, "Dost thou think, because thou art virtuous, there shall be no more cakes and ale?" This last aspect of Puritanism occurs very frequently in the articles against the clergymen of Norfolk and Suffolk who were summoned to appear before Manchester's committees. Most of them were accused of such grave offences as observing ceremonies, bowing to the altar, setting up altar rails, maintaining Bishop Wren's "popish innovations", or saying that "all were blockheads and beetleheads that spake against the crosse in baptisme". But quite a number had to face charges which arose directly from the Puritan dislike of pleasure and harmless recreation, and of which Mr Playters's "scandalous eating of custard" was an extreme instance. If they enjoyed a game of cards or skittles they were denounced as gamesters. If they liked to entertain their friends and to be entertained by them, they were gluttons, wine-bibbers, alehouse-haunters.

The Rev. William Proctor of Stradishall, for example, was said to permit card-playing in his own house, with "four paire of cards goeinge at one time". He also had "a paire of nine-holes" in his house, and encouraged his parishioners to make use of them. (What would these Puritans have thought of the present-day whist-drive, and the bowling for a pig at the village fête?) The Rev. Laurence Eachard of Yoxford was accused of keeping dogs, of hunting with them, and of frequently playing cards. He pleaded that he had not hunted for four or five years, and never played cards at all. The Rev. Nicholas Sherwood of Earsham favoured the playing of Sunday games, according to his adversaries, and refused to preach on Sunday afternoons, saying that "he who preached twice prated once". He also was charged with drinking and card-playing. So the denunciations went on in parish after parish; and almost without exception the accused clerics were ejected and their stipends sequestrated, with a small allowance grudgingly paid by the intruding minister for the support of their wives and children.

Many of them died in poverty; but some survived to be triumphantly reinstated in their livings after the Restoration. Amongst these was the Rev. Lionel Playters. He had undergone many unpleasant experiences since he was ejected, together with his wife and four children, from his parsonage at Uggeshall. He had lost his stipend; his small private estate had likewise been placed under sequestration; he had lost 200 pieces of gold, which he had hidden in the grave of one of his children in the chancel, and which "these godly reformers" had discovered when they were tearing up the altar rails. But in 1660, like his King, he came into his own again; and he lived in high prosperity for nineteen more years, transmitting his title and his estates to his son Sir John Playters, who proved, in the words of Walker, "a Worthy Gentleman, and a True Friend to the Church of England".

THE WINTER RISING I

THE YEAR 1650 drew towards its close in an atmosphere of bewilderment and unrest. At the end of 1648, Pride's Purge had deprived the people of their lawfully elected government. At the beginning of 1649 the judicial murder of the King had horrified the nation as a whole, and dismayed many of those who had been most strenuously opposing him a few years earlier. In the words of an unidentified Norfolk writer of the time, "the people of England, groaning under the heavy burthen of their newly created taskmasters, were ready to lay hold of any opportunity whereby to be eased of their intolerable burthens, they being brought by sad experience to call to mind the happy dayes which they had enjoyed under kingly government, which compared with the arbitrary actings of the Regicides, now as statesmen reigning, their little finger appeared to be more heavy than were the King's loynes".

In Norfolk this widespread discontent found expression in a rising against the established power, which was quickly and ruthlessly suppressed. So far as I know, only a few fragments of first-hand evidence about the affair have survived. I have tried to piece together the scanty and sometimes confusing details, and to present a narrative of what seems to have occurred.

In the latter part of 1650 a number of people in Norfolk "complotted to adventure their all for the interest of their royall master". It was a popular movement, in which the Royalist gentry, hopelessly outnumbered by their Puritan neighbours and crippled by fines and sequestrations, played no open part. Almost without exception the conspirators were tradesmen, husbandmen and artisans. One of the most active figures among them was a man sometimes known as Smith and sometimes as Kitchingman, who rode about the countryside urging everyone of known Royalist sympathies to take part in the intended rising. A rendezvous for a certain night at the beginning of December was arranged on Easton Heath, where a large body of Royalists was to assemble and march to Norwich. A party of supporters among the citizens would be ready to open the gates to them; and with Norwich in their power, the revolt would spread far and wide.

It was a wildly ambitious scheme, and it failed completely. On the appointed night groups of Royalists made their way to Easton Heath, especially those from around Mattishall and Dereham; "but the company was nothing answerable to expectation". Someone had warned the authorities at Norwich, who were on the alert; and the little company on the heath eventually dispersed, some going back to their homes and some into hiding. No arms were drawn, no blood was shed. That was the whole of the rising.

The Commonwealth authorities, however, took the gravest view of this pathetic little demonstration, or rather of the strong popular feeling which lay behind it. For some while they had been expecting trouble in Norfolk, and a large number of troops had been stationed in various parts of the county. The scattered Royalists were rounded up and clapped into prison. It was solemnly proclaimed that a most dangerous insurrection had been nipped in the bud. The prisoners learnt that their comrade Smith, *alias* Kitchingman, had all the time been "a decoy ducke to drawe in all the Royallists into the Usurper's nett"; he divulged all their plans and all their secrets, and on his denunciation many other supporters of the King were sent to gaol. It was decided to make an example of these conspirators which would strike terror throughout Norfolk and far beyond.

Prominent among the organisers of these measures was Colonel Robert Jermy, the Puritan squire of Bayfield, near Holt. A Royalist song depicted him thus:

> *He's a Journeyman Soldier to the State's Army.*
> *And 'tis in his terms, When you fight you must spare me;*
> *So runs the Commission of Colonel Jermy,*
> *   If I be informed true.*

> *Upon a Mock-Larum he's sure in the Van,*
> *Where he takes none and does no more hurt than he can;*
> *He's a pittiful Soldier, though a cruel Man,*
> *   Let's give the Devil his due.*

A letter from Jermy to William Lenthall has survived, couched in typical Puritan phraseology, giving the official version of what had occurred. "In the first outbreaking of this insurrection the whole country seemed in a flame—and had been, had not the Lord, even in the moment appointed for your and our sure overthrows, showed he was God, our God, who hath saved and would not now forsake us. They had so many parties appointed and in so many places that we could apprehend no place safe; but our fears were soon past, through the certain information they were all scattered and gone. They fled for fear of pursuers, but none pursued them but the terror of their own fault." He then suggested how the prisoners should be dealt with. "This is too plain, that many, yea we justly fear so many of the middle ranks of men are engaged in it, that it will be no end to try them by jury, but either to make some exemplary by a martial trial, or by the High Court of Justice." His suggestion of a special High Court of Justice was adopted. A Royalist account asserts that it was feared that a jury would not convict their fellow-countrymen on such a charge, and that therefore the Court was "by the predominant power of the Rump of the Parliament erected on purpose for the butchering of those persons".

THE WINTER RISING II

THE SPECIAL HIGH COURT OF JUSTICE first met at Norwich, with a great deal of pomp and ceremony, on 20th December. It was composed of three Judges, "most eminent friends to that tyrannical power", together with several prominent local supporters of the Commonwealth. Special relays of horses brought the Judges down from London, and the High Sheriff, Hugh Audley of Old Buckenham, was ordered to provide an impressive bodyguard for them. He appears to have failed in this or some other function, for a few days later he was fined by the Court "for neglect in performing the duties of his place". On the second day the Court condemned to death four Norwich men, William Wilson, Nathaniel Bennet, William Trott and Edmund Brady. (Another account adds two more to their number, David Purslew and Robert Betts.) Presumably these were some of the conspirators who were going to open the gates of the city to the main body marching from Easton Heath. They were hanged in Norwich Market Place two days later, "and dyed very couragiously, crying out on the gallows, 'God Save the King', and saying to this purpose, 'That, whereas they stood condemned by the Judges to dye as traytors, they were innocent and true subjects, and the Judges were the traytors'." For the whole of the following week, which included Christmas Day, the Court, "being both Judges and Jury", continued to try the unlucky Royalists, until at least twenty had been condemned to death. Two more were executed at Norwich, two at King's Lynn, two at Downham Market, two at Swaffham, and one each at Thetford, East Dereham, Holt, Fakenham and Walsingham.

Almost all the victims came from what Colonel Jermy described as "the middle ranks of men"; and to his sincere disappointment "those of power and eminency" had held aloof. But the authorities were anxious to make the conspiracy appear as widespread and dangerous as possible, and had managed to secure "one black coat and one red coat, meaning one minister and one gentleman, to suffer among the rest". The minister was the Rev. Thomas Cooper, and the gentleman was a young man named William Hobart. They were both closely connected with Holt, and it was thought that the fate of both was attributable to the zeal of Colonel Jermy.

> *To sacrifice to his Fears and his Pride,*
> *He caus'd a Church-Champion to be murder'd and try'd,*

ran the song from which I have already quoted; and there can, I think, be little doubt that it was so.

Thomas Cooper was born at Edgefield, and in 1631 became Rector of Little Barningham. He was presumably ejected from his living on political grounds early in the Civil War, since in 1643 he appears as an usher at Holt School, a position which he seems to have managed to hold until his death. In accordance with a particularly disagreeable Puritan custom, the Judges made a point of trying him on Christmas Day, "partly to show their dislike of the observation of that day, and partly to add to his affliction, whom they well knew to honour that festival day". It was alleged that they persuaded young William Hobart, by promises of leniency, to testify against him. He was duly condemned, and was executed shortly afterwards, probably outside the door of the Grammar School at Holt.

The case of William Hobart was perhaps even harder. His father, James Hobart, was lord of the manor of Holt, and the head of a junior branch of that widely-ramified family. Their more powerful kinsmen at Blickling and Intwood had been very active on the Parliamentarian side throughout the Civil War; and Sir John Hobart of Blickling was soon to become a member of Cromwell's short-lived House of Lords. But the Hobarts at Holt were obstinately Royalist, and both James Hobart's sons, Edmund and William, became involved in the rising. If it was true that William Hobart testified against Parson Cooper, it availed him nothing. He also was con-demned, executed in the market place at East Dereham, and buried at Holt on 4th January 1651.

Great efforts were made by Hobart's family to obtain a reprieve, and eventually the members of the Court voted as to whether the sentence should be carried out or not. Rumour said that the decision would have gone in Hobart's favour but for a mistake made by Matthew Lindsey, the Mayor of Norwich, one of the associate Judges, who, "not understanding the terms of the question, being put obscurely, as whether he was *pro* or *con*, voted for Hobart's death when he intended to vote for his life". The poor Mayor afterwards explained his error, but the presiding Judge would not allow the verdict to be altered, "which awoke Mr Lindsey into soe sad an apprehension of his mistake, as that about a fortnight after he fell sick and died". Whatever the cause may have been, he did in fact die later in the month.

The elder brother, Edmund Hobart, managed to escape the troopers who were in search of him. He was befriended by Anthony Riches, a currier of Holt, who hid him for three days in the roof of his wood-shed. Then he made his way to London, and lived in disguise as a servant in the house of a shoemaker. Several months later, when the storm had died down, he surrendered, and was eventually discharged under a heavy bond on condition that he took the oath of loyalty to the Commonwealth. He remained in London, greatly impoverished, until the Restoration; and although some of the tales of his adventures are probably exaggerated, docu-ments exist to show that he continued to work as a shoemaker for some years. There is a pleasant tradition that at the Restoration he brought with him to Holt the shoemaker who first employed him, and maintained his old master there to the end of his days.

His monument is still to be seen in the chancel of Holt church. It tells the visitor that Edmund Hobart died in 1666, "after he had escaped the Malice of the Usurper, who for his Loyalty to the Blessed Martyr King Charles I sought after his life and forced him from his paternall seat to live in Obscurity; but his Loyalty carried him steadfast through the storms of that unnaturall Rebellion, and here at last he found rest and expects a blessed Immortality".

THE CATHEDRAL IN DANGER

IN THE EIGHT CENTURIES and more of its history Norwich Cathedral has survived many dangers, from fire and gale and tempest, from the rioting of angry citizens, from the aerial bombardment of a hostile nation. But it was never in more continuous peril than in the seventeenth century, during the years of the Civil War and the Commonwealth. The system of church government had been abolished in England. All bishops, deans and prebendaries had been ejected, and their revenues were nuder sequestrian. Puritan iconoclasm had done its worst in cathedrals and churches throughout the land.

Bishop Hall of Norwich, in his tract entitled *Hard Measure,* painted a most vivid picture, too familiar to be quoted again here, of the desecration of his cathedral and the plundering of his palace. Sir Thomas Browne has added other details—how more than a hundred brass figures and inscriptions were torn from the tombs, how the great organ was broken up and burnt, and how the richly embroidered copes of the cathedral dignitaries were flung into the fire "with showting and rejoyceing". But even worse things might have happened. The entire building, in the eyes of many enthusiastic Puritans, was an idolatrous pile of valuable materials, stone and lead and timber, which might well be dismantled and put to more profitable uses. And in 1650 it seemed good to the authorities of Great Yarmouth that they should endeavour to secure such a prize.

So in May of that year the House of Commons was confronted with "the Humble Petition of the Bailiffs, Aldermen and Commonalty of Great Yarmouth in Common Council assembled". There was a long and obsequious preamble, full of typical Puritan cant— "our God hath broken the snare, and wee are delivered to praise his name, who hathe gathered together this Honourable House as so many choice arrowes into his quiver to smite through the heartes and loines of his and his people's enemies". The petitioners then prayed for some abatement of the monthly rate charged upon their town, "your late clemency to the Towne of Ipswich in the county of Suffolk raising our hopes to successe therein". Finally they begged that "you will be pleased to grant us such a part of the lead and other usefull materialls of that vast and altogether useless Cathedrall in Norwich, towardes the building of a works house to employ our almost starved poore, and repairing our peeres, or otherwise as you shall thinke fitt and sufficient".

What a revelation of the Puritan outlook at its worst is the phrase "that vast and altogether useless Cathedral"! Even the Corporation of Norwich, themselves equally Puritan in temper, might have resented such words from their Yarmouth neighbours. Little though they approved of episcopacy, they still listened to sermons in the Cathedral, delivered from a pulpit erected close to Bishop Overall's tomb, "with the Aldermen's seats at the east end, and the Mayor's seat in the middle at the High Altar". And if it was to be pulled down, had they no use within their own city for its materials? I do not know what form of answer Parliament may have returned to the petition; but the stones of the Cathedral were destined to build no pier or workhouse at Yarmouth. The splendid fabric stands essentially unaltered to this day.

But its fate may have hung in the balance nevertheless; and I think those who love the great building may owe a considerable debt of gratitude, hitherto unacknowledged, to a Norwich citizen named Christopher Jay. He was a leading member of the Corporation during the Commonwealth years, serving as Sheriff in 1653 and as Mayor in 1657; but he did everything in his power to preserve the Cathedral from harm, and spent large sums of his own money on its repair. In fact his private sympathies were all in favour of the Monarchy and the Church. At the Restoration he came into his own. He was elected for Norwich to the Cavalier Parliament in 1661, and his name was suggested as one of the Knights of the Royal Oak, an order which was never established.

He also felt himself entitled to some recompense for his services in the preservation of the Cathedral. I lately came upon a document in the Bodleian Library which shows that he made certain claims upon the Dean and Chapter, which were disputed by them; and that the matter was then referred by royal command to the arbitration of the Bishops of Lincoln and Exeter. The two prelates reported themselves satisfied that "the said Mr Jay in the late disordered times, when endeavours were used to demolish the Cathedrall Church of Norwich, had not only prevented the same, but disbursed considerable sums of money in the needfull repaires of that Church, which would otherwise have fallen into very great decay if not utter ruine". The King therefore commanded "that he should bee fully repaid those disbursements, with interest for the same and with an acknowledgment of his good service to the Church therein".

Mr Jay also had a disagreement with the Dean and Chapter over the lease of the manor and rectory of Hindolveston. Such a lease had certainly been granted to him in 1648 for a term of twenty-one years; but for some reason the new Dean and the reconstituted Chapter repudiated it after the Restoration, and granted a fresh lease to another person. The two Bishops declined to arbitrate on this question, "as being proper to the determination of Law"; and the King, while again "recommending the said Mr Jay to the favor of the said Deane and Chapter . . . with some respect to his former good services done for that Cathedrall", agreed to "leave the determination of this difference to the due course of Law", if an amicable settlement could not be reached beforehand.

I do not know whether the Dean and Chapter accepted the King's very strong hint, and granted Mr Jay the lease he desired. He continued to represent Norwich in Parliament until his death in 1677. It is sad but apparently true that after all his generosity on behalf of the Cathedral, he died a much impoverished man.

POUNDS, SHILLINGS AND PENCE

A BOOK upon which I have long been engaged has involved the examination of a great mass of seventeenth-century accounts. I have emerged from the task with a deeper respect than ever for our economic historians, who base their impressive theories and their formidable controversies upon just this kind of material. My own researches have had a more restricted scope, being concerned only with the story of a single estate; but I have come to feel very strongly the fascination of these account-books in their vellum or sheepskin covers, ranging in time from Queen Elizabeth to Queen Anne, and in fashion from elegant Italian script to the most crabbed and abbreviated hands imaginable. Rentals, manorial records, inventories, farming accounts, stewards' accounts, household and kitchen accounts—they all build up into history.

Of all these books, one of the most interesting and least complicated provides a record of the personal expenditure of John Windham of Felbrigg between 1654 and 1656. It was kept by two successive stewards, who were responsible for the multifarious day-to-day payments made on their master's behalf. John Windham is a rather shadowy figure in the story of Felbrigg, which he owned from 1654 until 1665. He took no part in public affairs; he married four wives, but no children survived him; there is no monument in the church to his memory. But during the three years covered by this account-book the quiet country life at Felbrigg jogged uneventfully on; and we can learn a good deal about that life, and even a little about John Windham himself, from its pages.

Some of the earliest entries refer to the death of his father Thomas Windham. Dr Browne, the future Sir Thomas, who had attended him in his last illness, was paid his fee of thirty shillings. The sexton received half a crown for "making the grave for my old Master", and ringing the bell. Later the sum of £8 15s. was expended on his gravestone. (The elaborate monument which commemorates Thomas Windham in Felbrigg Church was not erected until fifteen years afterwards.) But though owners may die, the life of their estates and households must go on. Besides the regular wages to various workmen whose duties are unspecified, there were payments for ditching and carting, thatching and tiling, threshing peas and cutting flags. Seven shillings were paid "to the Ratt Catcher for taking Ratts". The buttery boy had a new suit of clothes (7s. 9d.), a new pair of stockings (3s.) and a new pair of shoes (2s.). The footboy's clothes, evidently a rich suit of livery, cost £3 13s. 1d. Chimneys were swept (2s.), a key was required for the garden door (1s.), a copper cauldron was bought (35s.) and a table for the hall (15s.). Later three "Spanish tables" cost £2 8s. 4d.

There were, of course, endless purchases of provisions. Two pullets cost 1s. 6d., a side of pork 7s., 5 bottles of sack 12s. 6d., 5 pints of white wine 2s. 6d., 3 barrels of beer 33s., 4 crayfish 1s., "Crabbs and Crayfishes 27 in number" 4s. 10d. (I think these crayfish were really lobsters, a word never used in the book despite the nearness of Felbrigg to a coast whose lobsters have always been renowned.) There were payments of 4s. for oranges, 1s. 8d. for lemons, 6s. 8d. for pickled oysters, 19s. 6d. for a barrel of red herrings, 9s. for anchovies, 8s. for olives and capers, 6s. for sugar candy. And in July 1654 some sort of festivity took place at Felbrigg, perhaps connected with one of John Windham's marriages. On this occasion the purchases included 4 turkeys (2s. 10d.), 2 pigs (3s.), 10 chickens (2s. 6d.), 12 ducklings (4s.) and 7 dozen sparrows (1s.), while neighbours sent gifts of trout and capons, and Sir Horatio Townshend's man was paid 2s. 6d. for bringing a salmon.

Sport does not figure in the volume as much as might have been expected. A new fowling-piece was bought for 25s., and there are occasional entries about powder and shot. A pair of bells for the hawks cost 1s. and two hoods for them cost 8d.; but there are, I think, no records of the purchases of the hawks themselves. Again, half a crown was paid to "a man that brought the Beagles and Whelps from Kirbye"; but there is nothing about the use that was made of them. The "Phesant Howse" was newly walled in 1655— was this an aviary, or an equivalent of the "partridge mew" which produced birds for the table? A rather unexpected pet was a monkey, which a man was paid sixpence for "bringing home" to Felbrigg in the same year.

A few miscellaneous entries as one turns the pages—a firkin of the best soap 25s., combs and washballs 2s., a pair of spurs 1s. 6d., "a raspe to chipp the bread" 2s., "a sett of table men" (for a game of backgammon) 8d., "2 pair of Spanish leather shooes for my Master" 10s., "for mending my Master's watch" 3s. John Windham was evidently a great smoker; there is much about tobacco, tobacco boxes and tobacco pipes, which were bought by the gross and were of several grades.

No trace of the agitations of the Commonwealth years, no hint of Cromwell's bewildering series of experiments in government, has filtered through to these pages. Windham went to Norwich to cast his vote in the election of August 1656, and he and his party stayed at the King's Head, where the ostler was paid £1 12s. The only other suggestion of current events lies in the entries of large purchases of stone from the dismantling of Baconsthorpe, the mansion of the Heydons, whose impoverishment had been completed by their support of the King in the wars of the previous decade.

THE PARLIAMENT OF 1656

IN THE SUMMER OF 1656, wrote John Evelyn in his diary, "was a confus'd election of Parliament call'd by the Usurper". It was the third time in the Commonwealth years that a Parliament had been summoned; and it followed a period during which England had been subjected to the dictatorial rule of Cromwell's twelve *gauleiters,* the Major-Generals. The Lord Protector, in the words of Clarendon, "now thought his reputation, both abroad and at home, so good, that he might venture again upon calling of a Parliament; and by their countenance and concurrence, suppress, or compose those refractory Spirits, which crossed him in all places". He had been careful to appoint Sheriffs upon whom he could rely—Edward Ward of Bixley was that year's High Sheriff of Norfolk—and he expected them "to contribute to his designs, by hindering such Men to stand against whom he had a prejudice . . . and by procuring such Persons to be returned as would be most agreeable to him".

Up to the time of the Commonwealth, and again from the Restoration until the Reform Bill of 1832, the electoral pattern of Norfolk remained unchanged—two members for the county, and two for each of the boroughs of Norwich, Great Yarmouth, King's Lynn, Thetford and Castle Rising. But for the Parliaments of 1654 and 1656 the county was allotted ten representatives, while Thetford and Castle Rising were disfranchised—quite justifiably, since neither of them ever boasted more than 30 or 40 electors. In the 1656 election King's Lynn, which had been thoroughly brought to heel since its Royalist uprising in the Civil War, returned two of the Major-Generals, Skippon and Desborough. Yarmouth chose two reliable supporters of the régime, Charles George Cock and William Burton. The Norwich representatives were Barnard Church and John Hobart.

For the ten county seats there were 17 candidates. The despotism of the Major-Generals had aroused intense resentment throughout the country; and although no aspirant to Parliament would openly have professed Royalist sympathies, there does seem to have been among the Norfolk candidates some sort of an opposition group acting in concert. A few weeks before the election Robert Wilton of Wilby, in a letter encouraging his brother-in-law, John Buxton of Tibenham, to be one of the candidates, had written: "The adverse party are and will be hard at work, plotting and contriving their game how to play it for their own advantage, having the High Sheriff to assist them." A different element of opposition was provided, in many parts of the country, by certain old Parliamentarians or "republicans" who abhorred Cromwell's absolutist tendencies, and believed him to be aiming at the Crown. One of these was John Hobart, the member for Norwich.

The voting for the county seats certainly seems to justify the adjective "confused" which Evelyn had applied to the election. A fervent Cromwellian, Sir John Hobart of Blickling, was at the head of the poll with 2781 votes. On the other hand Charles Fleetwood, Cromwell's son-in-law and the Major-General who had ruled over East Anglia, only scraped in by less than 200 votes over the first of the unsuccessful candidates. Between them came Sir William D'Oyley, Robert Wilton, Sir Ralph Hare, Philip Wodehouse, Sir Horatio Townshend, John Buxton and Thomas Sotherton, with Robert Wood just behind Fleetwood and the last of those returned. I speak with some hesitation, and indeed the whole of this article is open to correction by anyone who has studied the Commonwealth period in Norfolk more closely than myself; but I think all these candidates, with the exception of Wood and perhaps Sotherton, either belonged to or were in sympathy with the opposition bloc to which I have referred. And I think also that Sotherton, like John Hobart of Norwich, may have been a member of the other opposition group, the "republicans". As for the seven defeated candidates, I have not as yet identified most of them with any certainty; but they included Tobias Frere, who had sat in the 1653 and 1654 Parliaments, and was very much a supporter of the current régime.

The result of the election was a disappointment and indeed a blow to Cromwell. "Very many Members were return'd", says Clarendon, "who were Men of the most notorious malignity against him." When Parliament assembled on 17th September, the members of whom he particularly disapproved were not allowed to take their seats. Sir William D'Oyley described this proceeding in a letter to John Buxton, who had been unable to attend. He reported the Protector's opening speech in carefully non-committal terms, and continued: "As to our county, pray know that none of our knights, or any other person, is admitted into the House without a ticket, which is denied (and soldiers at the door to keep them out) to above a hundred and forty gentlemen, without any reason given; amongst them Sir R. Hare, Mr J. Hobart, Mr Wodehouse, Mr Sotherton, you and I are of the number that must not come there." Similarly, of the members for the county of Suffolk only three were admitted. "I will stay here some short time yet", D'Oyley concluded, "and if admission be given, I will do my duty, and if not I will return to my own house, and pray for a blessing on the endeavours of others." Shortly afterwards more than ninety of the excluded members, all the six from Norfolk among them, published a spirited remonstrance. No attention was paid to their protests, and most of them soon withdrew to their own counties.

It is outside the scope of this article to discuss the chequered history of the 1656 Parliament. It abolished the rule of the Major-Generals; offered the Crown to Cromwell, who refused it; and set up a new constitution, which included a House of Lords to be nominated by the Protector. The excluded members were allowed to take their seats in January 1658; but fifteen days later Cromwell dissolved the last of his Parliaments, with the famous words "Let God be judge between you and me!" Those Norfolk members who had not been excluded seldom figured prominently in its deliberations, but some of them did speak occasionally. Although Sir Horatio Townshend was not among those excluded, he does not seem to have taken any part in the debates. A young man making his first appearance in public life, he was privately sympathetic to the Stuart cause, and was biding his time. In due course he was to play a more influential part than any other man in bringing Norfolk over to the King. Sir John Hobart, on the other hand, readily consented to become one of "Oliver's Lords", an indiscretion of which he was often to be reminded by his Tory opponents during the political struggles of the next reign.

THE DEATH OF CROMWELL

ON THE AFTERNOON of 3rd September 1658, Oliver Cromwell died at Whitehall. The third of September had always been an auspicious day for the Lord Protector, the day which brought him victory at Dunbar and Worcester. But 1658 was a year of political trouble and private sorrow. In February he had dissolved his last

Parliament. The successes of his foreign policy, the Battle of the Dunes and the cession of Dunkirk in the early summer, were overshadowed by mounting debt and widespread discontent at home. In August he lost the best loved of his daughters, Elizabeth Claypole. Thereafter the darkness gathered swiftly round a saddened and weary man.

The news of his death reverberated through England. In the whole course of our history, there had never been anyone quite like the hero who

> *Could by industrious valour climb*
> *To ruin the great work of time,*
> *And cast the kingdoms old*
> *Into another mould.*

The disappearance of that overwhelming personality brought new problems to a sorely tried land. "The great work of time" had indeed been altered beyond recognition; but Cromwell's succession of experiments in government had brought no sense of permanency, no assurance of any established order. Well might the great bureaucrat Thurloe, the most able administrator of the Commonwealth, write to the Protector's son Henry in Ireland that "this stroake is soe soare, soe unexpected, the providence of God in it soe stupendious, consideringe the person that is fallen, the tyme and season wherein God tooke hym away, with other circumstances, I can doe nothing but put my mouthe in the dust, and say, It is the Lord."

For the moment all was quiet. Richard Cromwell succeeded his father, and Thurloe told Henry Cromwell that "it hath pleased God to give his highnes your brother a very easie and peaceable entrance upon his government. There is not a dogge that waggs his tongue, so great a calme are wee in." But no one supposed that this state of things could last, or that the amiable easy-going Richard would long be able to control the stiff-necked people of England.

In Norfolk, as elsewhere, the Lord Protector had had his well-wishers and his bitter adversaries. There were plenty of people, in all walks of life, who had been content with his rule. Some of the leading men in the county's affairs were bound to him by family allegiance or by private ties of gratitude. Sir John Hobart of Blickling, whose wife was the daughter of John Hampden, had accepted a seat in the lately formed Upper House. He was to be ridiculed as "one of Oliver's lords" by his Tory opponents throughout the political contests of Charles II's reign. Charles Fleetwood, a distinguished soldier who owned property in Norfolk, had married Ireton's widow, the Protector's daughter Bridget. During the brief rule of the Major-Generals his authority had been paramount in East Anglia. And there were three men in Norfolk, high in the enjoyment of offices and estates, who were to be excepted at the Restoration from the Act of Indemnity "for being Instrumental in the murther of the late King".

William Heveningham, the squire of Ketteringham, had sat every day in the court which passed judgement upon King Charles. Valentine Walton, Cromwell's brother-in-law and for many years the Governor of Lynn, had done the same; and so had Miles Corbet, the vindictive doctrinaire lawyer who sat in Parliament for Great Yarmouth. But they, unlike Heveningham, had also signed the fatal death-warrant; and for them there could be no forgiveness. Heveningham surrendered at the Restoration, and was sentenced to confinement for life. The others fled abroad. Walton died in exile. Corbet was kidnapped at Delft, brought back to England and executed at Tyburn.

But at Cromwell's death the Restoration was almost two years away; and his supporters, whether extremists or moderates, can have foreseen nothing of that dramatic reversal of their fortunes. What of his adversaries? There seemed little likelihood of the King's return, except in the eyes of the most sanguine Royalists. It was widely desired, but no one had any coherent ideas as to how it could be brought about. Besides the faithful old Royalists, the Pastons and Bedingfelds and L'Estranges, there were many in Norfolk who had once upheld the Parliamentarian cause and were now utterly disillusioned by the turn of events. There were still some who had sat with Cromwell in the Long Parliament, or fought beside him when he was an inexperienced officer like themselves, and had never for one moment envisaged the murder of the King and the establishment of a Lord Protector. They—or more often their sons—were to exert their influence on the young King's behalf when the opportunity came.

So Cromwell passed into history, and soon into popular tradition. His career gave rise to countless fables and legends, usually quite unfounded, all over the British Isles. Norfolk has its share of them, and very absurd they are. I prefer to think of a different reminder of his greatness, his grand-daughter Mrs Bridget Bendish, who was still one of the sights of Great Yarmouth in the days of King George

I. She was the daughter of Bridget Cromwell by her first husband Henry Ireton, and married a gentleman named Thomas Bendish, who died long before her. She cherished the memory of her grandfather, to whom she was said to bear a strong resemblance, with the deepest pride, and maintained to the full his political principles and his Calvinistic tenets. She owned and managed a salt-works at Southtown: and there, said one witness, "I have very often seen her, in the morning, stumping about, with an old straw hat on her head, her hair about her ears, without stays, and, when it was cold, an old blanket about her shoulders, and a staff in her hand: in a word, exactly accoutred to mount the stage as a witch in *Macbeth*; yet if, at such a time, she was accosted by any person of rank or breeding, that dignity of her manner, and politeness of her style, which nothing could efface, would instantly break through the veil of debasement which concealed her native grandeur, and a stranger to her customs might become astonished to find himself addressed by a princess, while he was looking on a mumper."

PARISH AFFAIRS

IN AN ENGLISH VILLAGE of the seventeenth century, a larger proportion of the male inhabitants took an active part in parish affairs than is usually the case today. There were a number of responsible offices to be filled—churchwardens, parish constable, overseer of the poor, overseer of the highways and so forth—which entailed a good deal of trouble and hard work for those elected or appointed to them. The management of parish lands and charities, and the general working of the manorial system, were likewise matters of intimate concern to all; and everyone regarded the parish church as the centre of local affairs, and took a deep interest in everything connected with it.

I have lately been looking through a manuscript volume relating to the west Norfolk village of Grimston, which gives many examples of this general participation in parochial business, and throws much light on seventeenth-century country life. The volume was first intended to contain the accounts of the "Task Lands", a property administered by trustees for charitable uses. But the rectors of Grimston also used the book as a repository for notes and jottings relating to the affairs of the church and parish; and these notes constitute its main interest at the present time. At some later date it passed into the archives of Houghton Hall, and the Marquess of Cholmondeley has kindly allowed me to make use of it for the purposes of this article.

Grimston was a large and populous village; its parish officers were numerous, and they took their duties seriously. Every year the inhabitants met on Easter Monday and chose two church-wardens, two questmen, two constables, two surveyors of the highways and two overseers of the poor. For more than thirty years their names are recorded in the book; one sees the offices passing to and fro between neighbours, and descending from father to son. Summaries of the churchwardens' accounts are also given each year; no doubt more detailed accounts were kept in another book. Notes of the receipts and disbursements of the "Task Lands" trustees are regularly inserted. The funds of this charity were put to all kinds of beneficial uses: the apprenticing of friendless children, the sale of corn and hemp to the poorer inhabitants at reduced prices in hard times, repairs to the church, the building of a new vestry, the purchase of a school-house, the increase of the schoolmaster's salary. This last may still have been insufficient, for John Brooksbank, who had been "esteemed upon triall to be a meet Schoolmaster to instruct the children of Grimston" in 1659, is recorded to have "lately deserted" his charge in 1660.

In the remainder of the book, all sorts of parish occurrences have been noted down by three clerics, Thomas Thorowgood, John Brokett, and Thomas Cremer, who were successive rectors of Grimston in the seventeenth century. In 1626 Mr John Thorowgood presented to the church "a faire carpett of greene for the Communion table, edged round about with a greene silke lace and silke fringe suitable, and a cushion for the pulpitt of the same colour with great greene silke knobs, and a large cloth with like silke fringe for the pulpitt". In 1631 Thomas Rodwell undertook to keep the church clock and bells in order, and ring the bell morning and evening, for thirty shillings a year, together with fourpence for every "soule peale" for an adult and twopence for a child. Special collections or "briefs" are frequently recorded, sometimes on behalf of parishioners whose houses were burnt or who had otherwise suffered misfortune, sometimes for objects of wider import. In 1642 the collection "for the relief of the English come out of Ireland"—

refugees from the terrible rising there—amounted to £7 3s. 8d.;
in 1670 the parishioners gave £4 0s. 10d. "to redeeme the poor
distressed captives out of Turkey"; in 1678 they could only afford
£1 5s. 10d. towards the rebuilding of St Paul's Cathedral.

In the sixteen-thirties, that period of strict churchmanship, there
occur a few copies of the licences by which the clergy might authorise
invalids to relax the austerity of their Lenten fare. "Memorandum
that Thomas Thorowgood Rector of Grimston according to the
Statute did grant licence to Robert Griffith to eat flesh in this
Lent, it apyring evidently that fish and Lenten diet was unwhole-
some for him being now neere 18 months afflicted with a quartan
ague."

This firmness of ecclesiastical discipline is well shown in an affair
which the rector wrote down in careful detail in 1629. Robert Ashly
had deserted his wife and gone away for several months with the
wife of his neighbour Andrew Winey; but in due course, "touched
with the conscience of his sinn, he left her companie, and about
the last Lent came to his owne habitation, purposing at Easter to
receive the blessed Sacrament. But knowing it was not sufficient
to humble himselfe betwixt God and his owne soule, unless he
asked forgiveness alsoe of the congregation, whome he had offended
by his foule transgression; he did upon that day, of his own accord,
immediatelie after sermon, come into the midst of the people,
in the fullest assemblie, sorrowfully confessing his sinn, desiring
Almighty God to pardon him, and earnestlie asked foregivness of
all the parish, who had received offense by his fault; he desired
them to pray to God for him, that He lay not these wickednesses to
his charge, and assist him for tyme to come, that he fall no more;
he craved then to be admitted to the holy Communion, being now,
as he said, in some good manner fitted thereto."

The matter was referred to higher authority; and in September
of the same year Ashly appeared at Lynn before Dr Corbet, the
Chancellor of the Bishop of Norwich, and was ordered to do public
penance in Grimston Church on the following Sunday. "This he
performed with many words and signes of humiliation and sorrow
for his offence, with a white sheet, a white wand in his hand, and
a paper of great letters, ADULTERYE, and uppon his knees begged
pardon of God and the congregation." His penance done, the sinner
was admitted once more into the fold, and might partake of the
Sacrament in the company of his friends and neighbours.

SIR CHRISTOPHER CALTHORPE

MOST OF US feel an instinctive sympathy for lost causes; and we respect those ardent spirits who continue to uphold such causes, long after they are hopelessly and irretrievably defeated. The flight of King James II in 1688, and the arrival of William of Orange and his royal consort, certainly raised some difficult problems of conscience; but I cannot myself believe that the vast majority of our forebears were unjustified in their acceptance of the new monarchs, or in their willingness to take the oaths required of them. All the same, let us honour such men as Sir Christopher Calthorpe, who refused every inducement to follow the example of his friends and neighbours, and persisted in his convictions until the end.

His father, James Calthorpe of East Barsham, was not a Royalist, as some writers have declared—carried away, perhaps, by his decidedly Cavalier appearance in the well-known engraving ascribed to Faithorne. Indeed he was High Sheriff of Norfolk in the fateful year 1643, when Royalist sympathisers were very differently occupied. But he took no active part in political life, and died in 1652. At the Restoration his eldest son Christopher, a youth of seventeen, was created a Knight of the Bath on the coronation day of King Charles II, and the Stuarts were to have no more devoted adherent in Norfolk. He was to all appearances a fortunate young man, with his two fine houses at East Barsham and Thorpland, and his rich manor of Fakenham. He married a Suffolk lady, Dorothy Spring of Pakenham, and had a typical seventeenth-century family of fourteen children.

Towards the end of the new reign came the great trial of strength between the Court and Country parties. In the general election of February 1679, Sir Christopher was one of the candidates of the Court party for the county of Norfolk, and was returned at the head of the poll. But the Lord-Lieutenant of Norfolk, the first Earl of Yarmouth, a vehement supporter of the King, had exerted his personal influence during the election to excess even by seventeenth-century standards; and Sir Christopher and his colleague were unseated on petition. A fresh election was held in May, but this time he was not returned. In August there was another general election; again he stood, and again he was unsuccessful. Three bitterly contested elections in a single year were enough to depress the spirits and exhaust the purse of the most ardent candidate. So far as I know, Sir Christopher never stood for Parliament again; and it is probable that the expenses of 1679 permanently injured his estate.

Less than ten years later came the Revolution, and the momentous question of the oaths. They brought deep perplexity to many clerics and many laymen. The leading non-juror in the county was the Bishop, William Lloyd; but only a small proportion of his clergy followed his example, which entailed the loss of all preferment, and consequently of the means of livelihood for those without private resources. Among the laity the principal non-jurors were Sir Nicholas L'Estrange and Sir Christopher Calthorpe; and as such they appear in 1696 in the letters of Humphrey Prideaux, presently to become Dean of Norwich, who made it his business to inform the government of everything that went on in Norfolk. After the discovery of a plot to assassinate King William III the oaths were tendered again to prominent non-jurors, who were required to pay a fine and give further security if they declined to take them. Both knights declined; but whilst Sir Nicholas paid his fine and gave security, Sir Christopher refused to do either, and was therefore taken into custody. In several letters Prideaux urged the government not to make a martyr of him.

"He is a man of strong zeal and weak judgement and totally bigotted to Toryisme", he wrote, "but one whom I reckon a harmlesse man and noe otherwise inclined to show his affection to the cause he is in but by suffering for it." Again, "he is a very religious, sober, good man, but of a very weake judgement, which misguides him into this folley to court suffereings, because he thinks he is in the right cause". And in a third letter: "He will suffer ten thousand deaths rather than doe anything which he thinks amisse; but he is soe prepossest of the illegality of takeing the oaths to his present Majesty that it is not all the world can turn him, and there is noe sufferings which he would not patiently submitt to rather than doe this thing." The non-juring temper could not be better described, in all its courage and its obstinacy.

The authorities would seem to have taken a tolerant view of the case, as Prideaux had advised; and it is unlikely that Sir Christopher remained long in custody. He returned to live quietly in his own neighbourhood, where he was regarded, to quote Prideaux again, as "one of the most inoffensive men that lives, and delights in nothing soe much as to doe good to all he can". But misfortunes gathered round him. Of his many children, all but four died early in life, and of these only two daughters were to outlive him. His means also appear to have seriously diminished during his later years. The phrase in the will of one of his daughters, "our sinking family", was sad but true.

Sir Christopher died early in 1718. On his beautifully lettered ledger-stone, in the main aisle of Fakenham Church, it is recorded that he was the last survivor of the sixty-eight Knights of the Bath created on that far-off day of rejoicing, when King Charles II was crowned. And in the chancel is a tablet to the memory of his grandson, namesake and only male heir, who died less than three years afterwards at the grammar school of Bury St Edmunds, the last of all his line.

BISHOP SPARROW

ANTHONY SPARROW was Bishop of Norwich during the last nine years of the reign of King Charles II. A Suffolk man by birth and a distinguished Greek and Hebrew scholar, he was ejected from his Cambridge fellowship during the Civil War, and remained in obscurity until the Restoration. Then his loyalty was rewarded with a series of preferments, and in due course he became Bishop of Exeter, being translated to Norwich in 1676. He published a number of sermons and other works, and presided over his great East Anglian diocese with care and dignity, although his later years were clouded by ill-health and the religious and political animosities of that stormy time.

I have recently come across two letters which in their widely different ways throw a little fresh light upon Bishop Sparrow's career. The first, among the Windham papers at Felbrigg, describes his arrival at Norwich after his appointment to the see. The second, in the great collection of Tanner manuscripts at the Bodleian Library, threatens in uncompromising terms to murder him.

The first letter was written to William Windham of Felbrigg by his mother, who had remarried a Mr Chamberlaine and was now living in Norwich. The arrival of a new Bishop was an event of great interest to her, as indeed to everyone in Norfolk, and she hastened to tell her son all about it. I have modernised her spelling, which like the spelling of most seventeenth-century ladies was so erratic as to be at times almost unintelligible. "'Tis no news," she wrote, "that the Lord Bishop is complimented and visited by all sorts. I did think you and Lord Townshend would have come and done as the most and best sons of the Church do. He is very courteous, obliging and kind to all. He has been presented with venison from several: he has been invited out, and feasted at Sir William D'Oyly's, and a great appearance of company there to accompany him, gentry and clergy, three tablefulls. He has gone to see the Mayor and Aldermen. His lady and daughters were with me yesterday, all very civil and well behaved. He is not severe in his place, but invites all by kindness. He ordains in public at the Cathedral, and has a Sacrament every month there. . . . He is pleased to see the elder and better sort come for example's sake. I hope you will not neglect it."

The political conditions of the time no doubt had some bearing upon Mrs Chamberlaine's pious anxiety that her son should "compliment and visit" the Bishop, and should not neglect to receive the Sacrament from his hands. Windham and his brother-in-law Lord Townshend both supported the Country party, soon to be known as the Whigs, who were constantly accused by their High Church opponents of dissenting sympathies, attendance at conventicles and so forth. He would be unwise, in his mother's view, to give a handle to those who might try to cast doubts upon his religious orthodoxy.

As the political divisions within the nation grew more acute, the kind and courteous Bishop had to contend with many difficulties. Alike by duty and by conviction he felt obliged to support the Court party, which was ably led in Norfolk by Robert Paston, Earl of Yarmouth, the Lord-Lieutenant. But the Country party, led by Sir John Hobart and Sir Robert Kemp, steadily gained ground; and from 1678 onwards the struggle was tense and bitter. Many letters survive from Bishop Sparrow to Archbishop Sancroft describing the local situation, complaining of "froward Mayors" and disobedient clergy, and lamenting that his growing ill-health prevented him from being more active in support of Church and King. One day in June 1678 a mysterious letter from London arrived at the Palace. "Doctor Sparrow," it began, "your dayes are short and narrow, your proceedinges very sharp, and beinge it is so I will kill you; in so doeinge I shall doe God good service, for it is not fitt you should live any longer. The day is fixt, repent and forbeare. It is not your traditions and ceremonies, contrary to the word of truth, will save you. Repent in time. . . ." So the stream of sancti-monious abuse flowed on, ending at last with a spate of ferocious epithets above the appropriate signature "S. Blood".

The letter was that of a fanatical madman, who might well have attempted to carry out his threat. Lord Yarmouth was informed; and it is characteristic of the hysterical feeling of the time that he promptly took into custody six "notorious dissenters from the Church of England living in Norwich", including the well-known Dr John Collinges, who for many years had been the trusted spiritual adviser of the Hobart family. These highly respectable persons were bound over in the sum of £500 each to appear at the next Assizes: and although the matter seems soon to have blown over, dispassionate observers cannot have felt that the Lord-Lieutenant's action was particularly helpful.

But there were few dispassionate observers in England in the year of the "Popish Plot". In fact the Bishop, old and ailing, was compelled to play his part in one of the harshest and most critical moments of English history. When a new Parliament was summoned next year—and there were three general elections within three years, with all their accompanying business and commotion—he found himself too exhausted to travel up to London; he sent certificates from Sir Thomas Browne, affirming that from a journey by coach "hee might find such afflictive and paynefull effects as might endanger his life, or at least shorten his dayes". In 1685 he was granted at last that "quiet Exit" for which he had so often sighed in his letters to the Archbishop, and was buried in the chapel at the Palace, where a fine monument still commemorates his virtues.

THE TROUBLES OF
SIR PETER GLEANE

IN THE LITTLE CHURCH of Hardwick stands the altar-tomb of Sir Peter Gleane and Dame Penelope his wife, with an inscription from Sir Peter's own pen. From it we learn that he served King Charles I throughout the Civil War, raising and arming two companies of foot at his own charge. Indeed he had served the Crown faithfully for more than forty years, and held every military office from a Lieutenant to a Colonel of Foot. He was a Lieutenant-Colonel in the Norfolk Militia, and a Deputy Lieutenant for the county; he was likewise a Colonel and Deputy Lieutenant for the city of Norwich. In his civil capacity he had been a Justice of the Peace for twenty years and more, and had twice been chosen to represent the county in Parliament. "In which several services for his King and Country he spent his strength and weakened his fortunes; and the wounds which that [sic] received were not healed in this year 1683."

One not infrequently comes across epitaphs in which the misfortunes of the deceased person are lamented by those who survive him; but it is rarer to find someone taking steps to inform posterity, while he is still alive, of the harshness of his earthly lot. Sir Peter had sat for Norfolk, in the Whig interest, in the two short-lived Parliaments of 1678 and 1681. Had these contests really so impoverished him that he must proclaim the fact in his anticipatory epitaph in 1683? He was the grandson of the rich Norwich merchant of the same name, who gave to St Peter Mancroft the magnificent gilt cup and cover, embossed with the story of David and Abigail, which is one of the most treasured possessions of that church. Had he dissipated all his grandfather's wealth in the service of Charles I, and in electioneering expenses in what virtually amounted to opposition to Charles II? It would seem that such was the case. For these, and perhaps for other reasons, the fortunes of the family were fast declining. Lady Gleane died in 1689, and Sir Peter in 1695. Three years later his son and successor, Sir Thomas, was confined for debt in the Fleet Prison, whence he addressed a most pathetic appeal for aid, being "in great misery and want and almost naked". The baronetcy, bestowed on Sir Peter in the glad days of the Restoration, finally became extinct in 1745.

I have been enabled to see three unpublished letters from Sir Peter Gleane, which throw some further light on his character and circumstances; and I am allowed to quote them here by the kind permission of their owner, Mr H. L. Bradfer-Lawrence. They were all written in the summer of 1677 to Robert Paston, first Earl of Yarmouth. Sir Peter had some property in the parish of Waxham, including a decoy. Seventeenth-century Norfolk, with its vast areas of undrained marshland and fen, was a paradise for wildfowl of every kind. Shooting, as a sport, scarcely existed. The only method of taking duck in any quantity was by some form of netting, or by a permanent decoy. The decoy at Waxham had been one of the earliest established in this country, and Sir Peter regarded its produce as an important part of his income. Unfortunately he was on bad terms with a Mr Leigh, whose property adjoined his own, and with a Mr Smyth, the tenant of the land; and these worthies sought to discomfort him by systematically frightening the duck away from his decoy. Quiet is absolutely essential for the working of these ingenious traps; and the stratagems of Sir Peter's adversaries were so effective that he sought the good offices of Lord Yarmouth, in his capacity as Lord-Lieutenant.

In the first letter Sir Peter merely complained of Leigh's "unkindness" in general terms. He had bought a marsh adjoining his own property, which Leigh also coveted. "His Purse, my Lord, was fill'd when mine was emptied; that makes him promise himselfe Conqueror, and boasts accordingly; the justness of my Cause I am well assured you will espouse, which will give mee Courage to receive his Attacques, who is not only Master of the sinnews of warr, but Law itselfe." In the second letter he went into greater detail. "I have, my Lord, upon my freehold a dequoy that has been there fortie years and above, which is a great eye sore to Mr Leigh and Mr Smyth, and they study all the ways possibly to distroye it. Mr Smyth first caus'd shooting in every corner about it to fright the fowle from it; when that would not doe, he sent his servants secretly in the morning, when the fowles came from their feed, to fright them out of the Quoy, one of whose servants my servant took in my dequoy." The man had confessed he was acting on Smyth's orders; and Sir Peter, with mistaken leniency, took no action against him, in the hope that he might have "more neighbourly doeings" in the future.

It was a vain hope. "Now Smyth finds out peopell for his purpose, that are not Christians, or that have no Christian names that I can learne, and therefore can make no use of the King's lawes to protect mee; and these are persons employed under the pretence of mowing fodder in the fenns fast by my Quoy, but they bringe along with them stones, and slinges to throw them into the dequoy to fright the fowle, and this did not only their buiseness in frighting away the fowle, but indangered the lives of my servants, who worke about the Quoy, and are in that feare, that upon their examination before a Justice of Peace, did confesse that they durst not follow their buiseness without a guard, so that I am forct to have other servants with Gunnes to guard them while they are about their buiseness. . . . My Lord, my Loyalty has left mee but a small estate, I contracting a greate debt in his Majesty's service: I should be glad to keep that littell I have. And beleeve mee, my Lord, although my Quoy is but a littel helpe to mee, yet that littel is greate when there is but a small Estate, and to take away my livelihood is hard for flesh and blood to indure." He therefore begged Lord Yarmouth to interpose the full weight of his authority. "You may prevent mischeiffe that may follow if he still goe on in this darke and pevish way."

In the third letter he thanked Lord Yarmouth for "the greate trouble you have taken in my private afayres, to compose a difference that would royle flesh and blood, and the progress your Lordship has made in it". He also had much to say by way of apology for not paying his respects to the Lord-Lieutenant at Oxnead. He is particularly anxious lest some enemy should impute this neglect to political motives, rather than to his indifferent health and "my naturall disposition that makes Company a Burden to mee". There were fundamental political differences between the two men, nevertheless; and even if Lord Yarmouth did succeed in settling this affair of the decoy, his kindness did not prevent Sir Peter from opposing and defeating his Tory nominees in the bitter elections which lay a few years ahead.

REPERTORIUM

THE *Posthumous Works of the Learned Sir Thomas Browne, Kt, M.D.,* is a curious muddle of a book. It was one of the more creditable publications of the bookseller who has come to be known as "the unspeakable Curll", and whose character and malpractices were pilloried for all time in the writings of Pope. As Sir Geoffrey Keynes observes in his bibliography of Browne, "the make-up of the book presents a thorny problem to the present-day bibliographer no less than to the contemporary binder . . . and it is difficult to find two copies with the leaves similarly arranged". Moreover, the numerous plates have proved attractive to collectors addicted to the pursuit of "Grangerizing", and it is rare to come across an unmutilated copy. I was therefore delighted a few weeks ago to obtain a copy which has fine impressions of all the plates, and whose collation agrees in almost every respect with that laid down by Sir Geoffrey.

In 1712, thirty years after Browne's death, Curll had acquired a miscellaneous collection of his papers from one of his relations; and he "hurried the book into the press" without consulting Thomas Tanner and other learned personages in Norwich, whose advice would have improved it greatly. Some of its contents were hardly worth publishing, such as the little discourse *Upon Reading Hudibras*, in which Browne contrived not to mention *Hudibras* at all. The only item of real literary value was the beautiful *Letter to a Friend*, which had already appeared in print. But the short tract on the urns discovered at Brampton, "not much more than a Furlong from Oxnead Park", made a useful if somewhat prosaic pendant to *Hydriotaphia*, and is of some interest at the present moment, when important fresh traces of Roman settlement are being investigated in the same area of Norfolk.

The most substantial of the new pieces printed by Curll, however, was *Repertorium; or, some Account of the Tombs and Monuments in the Cathedral Church of Norwich*. Browne had witnessed, during his earlier years in Norwich, the havoc wrought in the Cathedral by Puritan fanatics, the brutal and senseless iconoclasm so eloquently described by Bishop Hall. A great number of monuments, brasses and inscriptions had disappeared, whereby "the distinct Places of the Burials of many noble and considerable Persons had become unknown". He determined to make a record of all the monuments whose position was still remembered, an enterprise in which he was much aided "by John Wright, one of the Clerks, above Eighty Years old, and Mr John Sandlin, one of the Choir, who lived Eighty-nine Years, and, as I remember, told me that he was a Chorister in the Reign of Queen Elizabeth". He also included such of the monuments as had escaped destruction, and the new memorials which had been erected "since those unhappy Times". His record was no dry list of inscriptions and dates. We are indebted to it for many historical details which might otherwise have been lost—that people used to try their money on the great slab which covers Chancellor Spencer's tomb, upon which the chapter rents were also paid; that "during the late Confusion" the aldermen were provided with seats within the sanctuary, with the Mayor's chair

in the place of the high altar; and all about the elaborate arrangements for the open-air sermons in the "Green Yard", before the
disapproving Puritans did away with them.

The latest in Browne's list of the monuments was that to Dean
Astley, who died in 1681. A Mr Hase provided Curll with a continuation, including details of some monuments which Browne had
omitted. Curll also persuaded a number of people to adorn the
work with plates at their own expense. These are far from being
masterpieces of engraving, but some of them possess a historical
interest second only to Browne's text. One represents the truly
astonishing hearse, a towering structure covered with escutcheons
and flags, which was used at the funeral of Bishop Redman in
1602. Another depicts the stately monument of Sir James Hobart,
who was attorney-general to the first Tudor monarchs, a sort of
chantry chapel between two pillars of the north aisle. This was
evidently standing as late as 1712; but there are iconoclasts in every
century, and it has now vanished except for the tomb itself and a
couple of armorial fragments attached to the pillars.

Most interesting of all these plates, I think, is that which shows
the memorial to William Inglott the organist, who died in 1621,
painted on the surface of the great pier at the south-east end of
the nave. The paint has now flaked away badly at several points;
and until the other day, when I first compared this plate with the
memorial, I had never realised that a remarkable little picture once
occupied the lower portion and is still faintly visible beneath a mass
of blots and blurs. The form of the dead organist lies venerable and
dignified, his hands joined in prayer. Beside him stand Art and
Age—

> *His Fame flies farr, his Name shal never die,*
> *See Art and Age here crowne his Memory.*

Art is an almost bardic figure with an open music-book, Age is
recognisable by his hour-glass and his flowing beard; and each
holds a wreath above the tomb on which

> *... William Inglott, Organist, doth rest,*
> *Whose Arte in Musique this Cathedrall blest.*

The restoration of ancient paintings is always a controversial
matter; and problems of much graver import confront the Cathedral
authorities on every hand. But it would be pleasant if one day it
were found possible to renew the picture of William Inglott and the

symbolical personages who attend him, as some years ago kind hands restored the tablet to his Elizabethan predecessor Osbert Parsley,

> *Whose low Estate was blest with quiet Mind*
> *As our sweet Chords with Discords mixed be,*
> *Whose life in seventy and four Years entwin'd*
> *As falleth mellow'd Apples from the Tree.*

I do not think that any other Cathedral contains similar monuments to its organists of three and four centuries ago, and there can certainly be none with inscriptions of greater originality and charm.

THE
EIGHTEENTH
CENTURY

THE LAST OF THE BLENNERHASSETTS

IN THE CHURCH of Caister-on-Sea, low down in a corner behind the font, is an inscription on a white marble tablet to the memory of John Blennerhassett, who died in 1704 at the age of fifty-two. It formed part of a very fine monument which was ruthlessly ejected from the church some time during the present century. Most fortunately, and unlike so many other victims of misguided "restorations", the whole monument was preserved by one of the parishioners. The inscription was subsequently replaced in the church; and it is now hoped that local piety may eventually reinstate the monument in its entirety. I was shown its many fragments the other day—urns and columns, a pair of weeping cherubs, the crest (a fox sejant) and the coat of arms (a chevron between three dolphins embowed) of the Blennerhassetts of Frenze. It closely resembles, in every detail, the monument in Norwich Cathedral by William Stanton to the memory of Dean Fairfax, who died in 1702.

Who was this John Blennerhassett, the last of the Norfolk branch of his ancient line, and how did he come to be buried at Caister? His family had flourished at Frenze for centuries; and the little church there, so difficult to find and so well worth the finding, contains a series of their monumental brasses. Their name was always regarded as somewhat out of the ordinary, and as far back as 1473 young Sir John Paston, who was some sort of cousin of the family, made fun of it. "Raff Blaundrehasset wer a name to styrte an hare." They sometimes used the alternative spelling Bleverhassett; and the name is often found, all through the centuries, in the abbreviated form of Hassett or Haysett.

In the earlier part of the seventeenth century their fortunes began to decline. They departed from Frenze, and lived in a large house at Pockthorpe on the outskirts of Norwich, which they leased from the Dean and Chapter. Long after their day it was still known as "Hassett's House", and was popularly supposed to be haunted by their ghosts. Dead bodies rolled across the rooms; there were sealed doors, and people were struck blind if they attempted to open them; the frequent apparition of "old Mr Hassett", in his coach driven by a headless coachman and drawn by four headless horses, dismayed the whole neighbourhood. The house was finally demolished to make room for the barracks at the end of the eighteenth century.

In the reign of King Charles II the family consisted of three brothers, Augustine, Edward and John. We learn something of Augustine from the letters of Sir Thomas Browne, whose patient he became in 1679. Sir Thomas wished him to consult his son, Dr Edward Browne, and other specialists in London. "Mr Augustine Blennerhaysett or Mr Haysett of this country" was, it appears, "eldest sonne unto Mr Haysett, and his father had been dead many yeares". He lived "at his house by Pockthorp gates", had recently decided to marry, and had "settled affection upon a good gentle-woeman". Unfortunately, marriage was just then an inadvisable step for him to take, for compelling medical reasons; so a consultation had been proposed with the younger Browne and his London colleagues. Sir Thomas went on to tell his son that Mr Blenner-hassett was "very jealous and apt to be meticulous, and hypochon-driacal". Nevertheless "hee is a kind gentleman and not intemperate, at least not of late". Furthermore "hee is a fayre conditioned gentle-man and hath a prettie good estate and not likely to be ungratefull, wherefore bee carefull of him and kind unto him and tender to answer his doubts, and not to discourage him".

We hear no more of Augustine Blennerhassett, or the results of the conference in London, or whether he married his good gentle-woman. If so he had no family, and he was succeeded in the occupation of "Hassett's House" by his brother Edward. The youngest brother, John, was married in 1687 to Elizabeth, daughter of John Rowe, Alderman and twice Bailiff of Great Yarmouth. John Rowe lived at Caister, and is buried in the church. The parish register records his burial in 1678, and that of Edward Blennerhassett in 1702, and that of John Blennerhassett in 1704. Evidently John moved to Caister on his marriage, and was joined in due course by his only surviving brother; and there the Norfolk branch of the family came to an end.

The inscription speaks of his retired life, his amiable character, his conjugal virtues, the exemplary performance of his religious duties. It refers also to the ancient lineage of the Blennerhassetts, and their distinguished family alliances. He had brought with him to Caister "an ancient canvas", on which all these illustrious matches were painted, with the name of the family inscribed beneath each coat of arms. After his widow's death this treasured object passed to her sister Mary, who had married a Mr Hill, and who also has a memorial in the church. It was in her house at Caister that Francis Blomefield saw the painted canvas, disposed around two rooms, and noted down the details for his *History of Norfolk*. But it had been hung against damp walls, and several of the coats were quite illegible. Mrs Hill died in 1737; and with her disappeared this last sad relic of the former grandeur of the Blennerhassets.

HENRY CROSS-GROVE

IN THE AUTUMN OF 1951 we celebrated the 250th anniversary of the first appearance of a newspaper in Norwich, and felt additional pride in the fact that Francis Burges's *Norwich Post* was the first newspaper in this country to be published outside London. The memory of Burges was honoured as his courage and enterprise deserved; and some reflected glory also fell on the other pioneers of journalism in Norwich, and among them upon Henry Cross-grove. The *Norwich Gazette* was established in 1706, when Burges's early death encouraged more than one competitor to enter the field. Cross-grove was brought down from London by its proprietor to act as editor; in due course he himself became the proprietor, and he remained in Norwich, a lively and at times a controversial figure, until his death almost forty years later.

The *Norwich Gazette* strenuously upheld the Tory cause, and Cross-grove was a staunch and vociferous Tory to the end of his days. He was in his element throughout the bitter political struggles of Queen Anne's reign; and when the Whigs emerged victorious at the accession of King George I, and the Tories entered upon their long period of eclipse, the *Norwich Gazette* carried on undaunted. Its editor even had to undergo some degree of political martyrdom, which he obviously rather enjoyed. Early in the new reign a petition was drawn up for silencing his press. He wrote with pride that "it was, I hear, signed by the Mayor, several Justices of the City, the High Sheriff of the County, and our good Dean, who all swim in the same stream; so that I am in expectation of being taken into custody of a messenger; but I am prepared for the storm, and so but little heed of it". Later in the year an indictment was preferred against him on charges of treason, "on all of which I am as perfectly innocent as the child unborn—but I have been too forward in expressing my approbation of monarchy and episcopacy, and in lashing such as I believe their enemies". The charges were in fact clearly frivolous, and he was honourably acquitted at the next Assizes. The *Norwich Gazette* continued upon its noisy and out-spoken career.

In the arts of publicity and self-advertisement Gross-grove was in advance of his time. Among other novelties he started in his news-paper a sort of "Answers to Correspondents" feature, inviting all kinds of conundrums from his readers and replying to them in his own peculiar strain, half learned and half facetious. This proved so popular that in 1708 he published two booklets, *The Accurate Intelligencer* and *Apollinaria*, which he described as "a very choice Reserve of such Questions as were too long or improper to be inserted in a Newspaper, some in Divinity, Philosophy, Poetry, History and Love, being Profitable and Pleasant". These little pamphlets, originally sold for threepence apiece, are now among the rarest of Norwich-printed books.

The *Norwich Gazette*, like the *Eastern Daily Press* today, attracted a wide variety of correspondents: indeed, comparisons might be drawn between the more prolific contributors to our familiar daily column and their predecessors in the reign of Queen Anne. But Cross-grove's answers really provide the entertainment of *Apollinaria*. As in political life nothing could daunt him, so he refused to be defeated by the extraordinary questions with which his readers flooded his printing-office. Scriptural conundrums were the most frequent; and he gave authoritative decisions about the repopulation of the world after the Flood, and Jephthah's vow, and the writing on the wall of Belshazzar's palace, and many another perplexing passage. In the realms of metaphysics, in the vast field of history, he was likewise omniscient. Some of his correspondents addressed him in verse, and in verse he replied to them. To questions of an unseemly nature he did not always feel obliged to give a more seemly answer. And he loved a joke. Someone wrote from King's Lynn to ask him "whether you think those People we call Cunning Men do really conjure, and that they can raise Winds, and raise the Devil when they will?" Cross-grove replied with relish: "If there could be such Creatures, NORWICH would certainly produce them; for there never was a Place more generally stocked with Scholards, Wits and Urania's Babies, Asstrologers I mean; and yet I can assure you here is not one in the City that is more of a Conjurer than Gaffer Gover's Ducks." The meaning of the last allusion is now, I suppose, lost in the mists of time.

Cross-grove was clearly a man of ability and intelligence; but he enjoyed playing to the gallery, he was violent and excitable in life as well as in print, and there was always more than a touch of extravagance about his various enterprises. Even when his wife died in 1742 his grief had to be conspicuously exhibited to the public gaze. Normally the *Norwich Gazette* appeared with a woodcut heading, a panorama of the city with its churches and houses tightly packed within the ancient walls, and the Cathedral and Castle towering above them. On this sad occasion the next issue appeared with a special heading, a most lugubrious display of skeletons and winding-sheets, figures of Death and Time, coffins and hour-glasses and every other emblem of mortality. The paper records that she was buried in St Giles' Church at 11 o'clock at night, a highly unconventional hour for such a ceremony. And there is the same unmistakable air of extravagance about the inscription, in flowery and idiosyncratic Latin, upon the ledger-slab in that church which still commemorates Judith Cross-grove and her devoted husband, "Typographus Norvicensis", who was buried by her side two years later.

A NORFOLK POLL BOOK

ELECTION CONTESTS have for several centuries formed a part of the life of England, and have often been reflected in English literature. One thinks of Dickens's incomparable picture of the goings-on at Eatanswill; of Peacock's description in *Melincourt* of the choosing of a representative for the ancient and honourable borough of Onevote; of episodes more seriously handled by Disraeli and Trollope and many other writers. I propose however to discuss a very different kind of book, a small eighteenth-century volume which at first sight contains nothing more than endless lists of names —the record of how the freeholders of Norfolk voted in the memorable election of 1734. Until the introduction of the secret ballot, which only took place some ninety years ago, these poll books were published as soon as possible after each election. It is easy to imagine how carefully they were studied by the candidates and their agents, and indeed, by anyone who was inquisitive about the political convictions of his neighbours. Even now, when the issues are dead which were once so burningly alive, when the tumult and the shouting have been stilled for all these years, they hold a curious fascination for the student of history.

Until 1832 the county of Norfolk, like all other English counties large or small, returned two Knights of the Shire to Parliament. Our five boroughs—Norwich, Great Yarmouth, King's Lynn, Thetford and Castle Rising—also returned two members apiece; so that Thetford and Castle Rising, typical "pocket-boroughs" with the merest handful of electors, enjoyed precisely the same representation in Parliament as the great county of Norfolk and the great city of Norwich. A voter resident in a borough had only to walk a few hundred yards to the polling booths; but all the county electors had to declare their votes in Norwich. This often involved what was then a considerable journey; and many of the freeholders expected the candidates and their wealthier supporters to defray their expenses, or at any rate to provide free food, drink and lodging for themselves and their horses during their stay in Norwich. Inns were opened to all comers at the charge of the candidates; and in most counties these and other heavy expenses caused the opposing parties to avoid a contested election if there was the smallest chance of a compromise. In Norfolk the Whig and Tory factions managed to adjust matters with great success during most of the eighteenth century. Contests might rage in Norwich; outsiders might assail the well-entrenched Walpole and Townshend interests at Yarmouth and Lynn; but a freeholder in the county might pass almost an entire lifetime without recording his vote.

After the triumph of the Whigs following the death of Queen Anne, there was no election in Norfolk for twenty years. Things settled down everywhere into a peaceful and prosperous routine, and in this county the parties agreed to return one Whig and one Tory to a succession of Parliaments. But in 1734 the country was beginning to grow weary of Sir Robert Walpole's long administration. At the general election in that year the Whigs and Tories in Norfolk could no longer reconcile their differences, and decided upon a trial of strength. For some years the Tory member had been Sir Edmund Bacon of Garboldisham, and he was nominated again. His Whig colleague had been William Harbord of Gunton; he now retired from the fray, and his nephew William Morden was adopted in his place. The other candidates were William Wodehouse of Kimberley for the Tories, and Robert Coke of Holkham for the Whigs. It is pleasant that the names of all four candidates (since William Morden later assumed his uncle's name of Harbord on succeeding to his property) are still very much alive in the county today.

The contest excited interest far beyond the boundaries of Norfolk, since Walpole, the long-established Prime Minister, was being openly challenged in his own native county. The struggle was long and bitterly fought out; frantic efforts were made to bring every possible freeholder to Norwich, and in the end 6302 of them came to the poll, a greater number than in any previous Norfolk election. Before me lies a copy of the poll book, a small quarto printed in good clear type on excellent paper, in which their names are recorded. They are listed under their towns and villages, and opposite each man's name the candidates for whom he voted are indicated. It must be remembered that the qualification for a vote was the ownership of freehold property of a minimum value of forty shillings a year; so that in parishes where most of the land was in one ownership, or was copyhold and not freehold, the number of voters seems surprisingly small. Taking a few parishes at random 83 freeholders voted from Wells, 46 from Diss, 43 from Attleborough, 29 from Holt, 27 from Swaffham, 26 from Docking, 23 from Fakenham, 20 from Aylsham, 9 from Catton, 2 each from Sprowston, Brundall, Hellesdon and Postwick, and only one apiece from Horsford, Costessey and Heigham.

Some towns and villages were much divided in their voting, others showed a remarkable unanimity. All the 15 freeholders from Sheringham voted Whig, and all but one of the 31 from Cromer; among the 83 from Wells there were only two Tories. On the other hand at Hingham all but three out of 57 freeholders voted Tory, and both Attleborough and East Dereham showed an equally decisive Tory majority. Fakenham and Swaffham were almost exactly divided between the two parties; and a very close division existed between those who resided in Norwich, but owned freehold property in the surrounding countryside for which they were entitled to vote.

Among so many forgotten names one occasionally comes across a name which is still remembered. Our historian, the Rev. Francis Blomefield of Fersfield, voted for the Tory candidates; but the Rev. Charles Parkin of Oxborough, who was to continue the work after Blomefield's death, voted for the Whigs. Sir Benjamin Wrench, the great physician of the day, and the Rev. Edmund Nelson, whose grandson was to make the name so illustrious, also supported the Whig interest. Henry Cross-grove, mentioned in a previous Essay as one of the earliest printers and newspaper proprietors of Norwich, was still true to the convictions which he had so vigorously asserted in former years, and voted Tory in respect of a freehold which he owned at Old Buckenham.

And the outcome of it all? Both the Tory candidates were returned, Bacon by a comfortable lead, Wodehouse only beating Morden by the narrow margin of six votes. The Whigs were bitterly disappointed, and did not readily accept their defeat. Doubtful votes were scrutinised, a petition was set on foot against Wodehouse's return, and there was an immense amount of wrangling and ill-feeling. A few months later Wodehouse died; but the Whigs finally decided against the expense of another contest, and his brother Armine Wodehouse was returned in his stead. At the next general election, in 1741, the county of Norfolk reverted to its accustomed and eminently sensible practice of electing one Whig and one Tory to Parliament without a contest; and the freeholders were not required to journey to the polling booths again until 1768.

THE DIARY OF JOHN IVES

I AM WRITING THIS ARTICLE on the other side of the Atlantic, from a village in the heart of Connecticut. The famous colouring of the New England autumn is beginning to show in the trees and undergrowth; and in a few more days the vivid scarlets and brilliant yellows will be blazing out from oak and maple, sumach and dog-wood, until the whole countryside seems aflame. The neighbourhood is rich in houses of the eighteenth century, mostly small in size but of great architectural beauty, their cool white paint contrasting delightfully with the riotous colours of the trees. The names of the towns and villages recall the original settlers of the country and the places in England from which they came. East Anglia is gener-ously represented, which is not surprising when one recalls the number of emigrants from Norfolk and Suffolk who sought their fortunes in America, for religious and other reasons, in the course of the seventeenth century. A few miles away lie Norwich and

Suffield and Wymondham (it is spelt Windham here); and across the border in Massachusetts are Yarmouth and Lynn, Attleborough and Hingham, Framingham and Walpole and Raynham.

The house in which I am staying contains one of the most remarkable private libraries in the world. It is fabulously rich in eighteenth-century material, and above all it is famous for its collection of the writings of Horace Walpole and the books from his own library at Strawberry Hill. One of Walpole's minor correspondents was the Yarmouth antiquary John Ives, who died in 1776 at the early age of twenty-five. Walpole acquired many of his manuscripts after his death. The other day, looking through these papers, I came upon a youthful diary of Ives's father, which had somehow got bound up with the solemn antiquarian correspondence of his son. This odd little relic of East Anglia, which has travelled so far to its final resting-place in Connecticut, provides an unexpected picture of life in Great Yarmouth through the eyes of a schoolboy more than two centuries ago.

The elder John Ives kept this diary from May 1734 until January 1736, when he was about fifteen years of age. He spelt badly but wrote clearly and well, adorning his margins and the ends of his paragraphs with neatly drawn lines in red ink. The diary opens with details of the voting at the hotly contested general election of 1734, when the Whigs were victorious at Norwich and Yarmouth, and the Tories carried the two seats for the county of Norfolk. Young Ives, incidentally, was a partisan of the Whigs; and later in his diary he copied a ribald song directed against the declining Jacobite sympathies of the Tory party.

> *Undone! undone! the Toreys cry,*
> *We are all quite undone:*
> *We can't have Jamey for our King,*
> *No, nor his eldest son.*
> *So Farewell then, poor James, they cryed,*
> *No fault with you we found,*
> *We strove our best to git you in,*
> *But now we are run aground . . .*

John Ives also noted the doings of the municipal dignitaries of Yarmouth, which at times were lively enough. For instance, on 29th August 1735 "a Dispute arose about the two Comisioners whear upon Mr Barry Love the preasant Mayor took Mr Nathaniel Symonds by the Nose, upon which he stroke him over the Head with his cane, and they held the Assembly till one a Clock in the Morning and then adjourned". Next day "the Gentilmen met again in a better mind" and settled their dispute about the commissioners.

Ives's father was a prosperous merchant at Yarmouth, and there are glimpses of the busy maritime life of the port on every page of the diary. There is much talk of the building of ships, the buying and selling of shares in them and in their cargoes, the time in September when the "cobels" began to unload their herrings in ever-increasing quantities, Dutch vessels coming into the harbour and the drunken brawling of their seamen. Sometimes worse things happened than drunkenness, as when "the news bring worde that Mr Ben Hart was stabbed in his cabon by the Ship's company and they intended to run away with the Ship and so go a Pirating".

As in most diaries there are plenty of christenings, marriages and burials, sometimes adorned with brief but pointed comments, as "Dyed Mr John Bird, he tooke one of Docter Ward's Pills." New clothes are often mentioned—a full coat, a new coat and breeches, silver sleeve-buttons, shoe-buckles and knee-buckles; and John Ives was also learning to dance. His favourite amusement was fishing; he used to catch smelts, butts and eels. His father liked to go "setting" in the country, but seldom brought back more than a brace of birds.

A rather surprising form of entertainment occurs in the spring of 1735, when "I and my father and brother went in our Chais to Gorlston to see a Man slide down from the Church Stepel, and pulled a barrow down with a Boy in it, and then an Ass flew down." The performance was repeated next week from the spire of Yarmouth Church, and a third time from the roof of a private house. On this last occasion the weights tied to the legs of the unfortunate ass were too heavy, and "pulled down the staging and the Ass tumbled down upon the Leads, but it did no Mischief".

In the Christmas holidays the family spent a few days at Norwich, where among other attractions there was a menagerie on show. The exhibits included "a white Bear, a Civet Cat, two Lepards male and female, two Panthers, a Marmoset, a Lyoness, a Dog with two Legs, a Hog in Armour [armadillo], a Crocadale, a Wolfe, a Camel, a Man Tyger, a Monkey, a Porpipine, a Jackel, an Ox". Filled with memories of this singular assemblage of creatures, John Ives returned to school at Yarmouth, and shortly afterwards the surviving fragment of his diary comes to an end.

THE MISSION TO CAWSTON

IN THE MIDDLE of the eighteenth century the people of Cawston were "strangers to morality—hateful and hating one another—seemingly given over to a reprobate mind—running to excess of riot—committing all manner of wickedness with greediness—remarkable, far and wide, for incivility to strangers". One hesitates to believe that conditions were ever like this in one of Norfolk's most agreeable little towns. The picture is no doubt much exaggerated; but the fervent evangelicals of two centuries ago were greatly given to exaggeration. The Rev. Thomas Bowman, the Vicar of Martham near Great Yarmouth, felt a call to rescue the people of Cawston from what he regarded as their deplorable state. Although his own parish was at least twenty miles away, he established in 1766 a congregation at Cawston, and ministered to its members continuously for a quarter of a century. When he retired from this work in 1791 he published a little book, *Caustoniana: or, Twelve Discourses addressed to the Inhabitants of the Parish of Cawston in Norfolk*, from which comes the above-quoted description of those inhabitants before they had enjoyed the benefit of his ministrations.

Until I recently acquired a copy of *Caustoniana*, I must confess that I had never heard of Mr Bowman. His discourses do not make cheerful or easy reading. But apart from the considerable amount of local information that may be gleaned from them, one cannot fail to be impressed by the audacity of the vicar of Martham in setting up this mission in a parish with which he had no concern at all. One wonders also how the legitimate incumbents of the parish can have regarded this enthusiastic intruder. The Rev. Leonard Addison had been Rector of Cawston for almost twenty years before the mission began; and when he died in 1772, his successor was the Rev. Richard Baker. What did Mr Addison and Mr Baker feel about Mr Bowman and his activities? One cannot suppose that they were very well pleased. Indeed in his preface Mr Bowman, without mentioning any names, refers to "envy, jealousy, malice and opposition of various kinds". On the other hand, he admits that the members of his flock, unlike similar congregations elsewhere, "have not been oppressed by the laws, have met no violence, have known no gross interruption while in the service of God". The probable disapproval of Mr Addison and Mr Baker would seem to have been tempered by the virtue of tolerance.

Unusual as this invasion of one clergyman's parish by another may have been, it was not altogether unknown. As Mr C. B. Jewson puts it in a letter to me, "Thomas Bowman was clearly an Evangelical first and foremost. To such men the Gospel was pre-eminent; the Church, as a visible structure, was of only subsidiary account." If he considered that the incumbents of Cawston were neglectful of their duties, or even insufficiently evangelical in outlook, his principles justified him in entering their parish. He must have led a strenuous life, travelling constantly between his own cure and the much larger parish which he had adopted. But his ministry was undoubtedly welcome. He mentions that his first meeting-place had to be enlarged, and that later, "by a very distinguishing Providence", a still more commodious building was erected.

Most of the discourses which he printed were occasioned by the deaths of members of his flock; and something may be learnt from them about the lives and activities, the virtues and the misdeeds of many Cawston people otherwise forgotten. Henry Roberson, "that dear man, whom I would call the father of us all", had been the earliest to support the newly-established mission, and was a pillar of strength and integrity. Ann Thorn, however, "imagining that our devotional meetings were improper, formed and openly avowed a design to disturb us when together, and actually came with that intent"—only to be speedily converted. Samuel Ward, who died at nineteen, was "uniformly steady and exemplary". Mary Fake, on the other hand, although she returned to the fold before her death at the age of fifteen, had for many months been "luke warm in her professions, and slothful in her practice".

There is a remarkable passage in the discourse upon Sarah Brooks, who died in 1790 at the age of 81. Many years before her death she dreamt that "a person in black came to Cawston and shewed the inhabitants, through a little wicket, to a place where they found better waters than the waters of Bawburgh. Her dream was not insignificant: for, a few weeks after, a person brought the message of salvation to Cawston, where it had not been heard for more than an hundred years." Mr Bowman was clearly much impressed by this vision, and by his own appearance in it as "the person in black". It is more interesting to us, perhaps, as evidence that even in the eighteenth century there survived outside Catholic circles a belief in the healing properties of Saint Walstan's well at Bawburgh, which had been regarded in medieval times with such particular veneration.

I can tell no more of Mr Bowman. He died in 1792, only a year after the publication of his book. A board in Martham Church records that his widow, on her death in 1816, left £300 with directions to distribute £2 yearly among the poor of the parish, the remainder to be laid out in educating six poor children. Mr Bowman's own memorial should be sought in *Caustoniana*. It must be a scarce as well as a forgotten book. Unreadable though much of it is, his ardour and sincerity are still suggested by the passages which describe the worldly troubles and the spiritual triumphs of those Cawston men and women of two centuries ago.

CROMER IN THE EIGHTEENTH CENTURY

THERE IS A GREAT FASCINATION in the parish and estate maps of the past, even the quite recent past. They often depict some familiar area of countryside, which now looks as if it had remained exactly the same for hundreds of years, in a startlingly different guise. The earliest examples reveal the common meadows, the great open fields, the innumerable little strips of land, all the features of a vanished system of agriculture. And even comparatively modern maps will demonstrate that the aspect of our land is perpetually changing—that boundaries and hedgerows are altered, heaths are converted into woodlands, roads constructed or disused, watercourses diverted, cottages demolished or regrouped. As Matthew Arnold wrote of the Oxford villages he loved so well:

> *How changed is here each spot man makes or fills!*
> *In the two Hinkseys nothing keeps the same . . .*

The words could apply to almost every parish in the land.

The older maps have an additional charm in the drawings with which they are so often embellished. The parish church, the mansion house, the farms and cottages are not indicated merely by ground-plans in outline. The cartographer preferred to represent them as they stood, and sometimes with great exactness. He would draw windmills and watermills, passengers and vehicles on the highway, husbandmen in the fields, cattle and sheep in the enclosures, boats on the rivers, fish in the streams and ponds.

Not long ago, through the kindness of a friend into whose ownership they had passed, I was given a set of maps of the estate which appertained in the eighteenth century to Cromer Hall. They were made in 1747 for Thomas Wyndham, who had lately inherited the estate from his brother, and who was, incidentally, my ancestor six generations back. They are beautifully executed, and adorned with drawings precisely of the type which I have described. One in particular presents almost a bird's-eye view of the town of Cromer, with every feature most skilfully depicted—the houses and other buildings, the streets, the orchards, the windmills, the hills which form its background.

High upon the cliff-top, and looking down upon a fine ship much too close to shore, stands the old lighthouse, long since vanished and replaced. At the northern end of Jetty Street two cannon represent the battery which defended Cromer from the dangers of invasion, sufficiently remote in 1747. The earlier Cromer Hall is clearly drawn, with its tall chimneys, its projecting wings and forecourt, its summer-house and fish-pond. Houses of varying sizes are scattered at intervals along a dozen streets, whose course has changed little in the intervening centuries, but from which other streets now radiate over a far wider area. Finally there is the Church, looking oddly truncated after the destruction of its chancel, and showing distinctly that portion of the chancel which it had proved impossible to destroy.

The demolition of the chancel had taken place in 1681. In that year the lessee of the great tithes, the Rev. Thomas Gill of Ingworth, claimed that it was too dilapidated for him to maintain, and sought the permission of the Bishop of Norwich to pull it down. The Bishop gave his sanction, and Mr Gill was allowed to sell the materials, on condition that he walled up the chancel arch and the eastern ends of the aisles. It is said that the chancel was blown up with gunpowder. Whatever the means employed, one substantial fragment of the arcade was left standing; and this appears not only in the map to which I have referred, but in the engraving of Cromer Church from a drawing made by Francis Blomefield in 1737.

This engraving shows the Church in a dismal state, with only the glorious tower presenting no conspicuous marks of decay. The fine windows in the south aisle are bricked up, with small lancets inserted in the brickwork. The western porch is a ruin. The entire roof appears to be sagging. Vegetation sprouts from the masonry. In fact, as we know from other sources, the upkeep of the great building was no longer within the means of an impoverished fishing-town.

By 1757 the Church had fallen into still worse decay, and there was even a suggestion that it might have to be demolished altogether. At that time the owner of Cromer Hall was Thomas Wyndham's son John, a very young man; and the advocates of destruction appear to have been checkmated by his older kinsman, William Windham of Felbrigg. In a hitherto unpublished letter to Windham from his former tutor Benjamin Stillingfleet, dated 8th February 1757, there occurs this passage: "I have been with the Bishop of Norwich and mentioned what you desired. He seemed glad that your letter came time enough to put a stop to the intended scheme against Cromer Church, and will not I am certain let anything be done without a thorough examination. I spoke much of the beauty of the building, and he agreed that it ought by no means to be destroyed if it was possible to keep it up. But I found he had been told that slate would not stand the force of the sea winds, and therefore you will do well to have this point considered particularly, by workmen who have had experience in that kind of covering."

Thanks to Windham's timely interposition with the Bishop, the Church was reprieved. Next year the eminent Norwich architect Thomas Ivory surveyed the building, and his recommendations and estimates have survived. He suggested a new roof of slate, "a neat flat ceiling to the middle isle", and many other necessary repairs, to the tune of £750, of which £490 might be recouped by the sale of the lead and some of the bells. Nothing was done for another nine years, so that by 1767 "the roof was chiefly fallen down, and the remainder, for preventing further damage, with great danger and expence have been taken down". The estimate for repairs had risen to more than £1000.

But now the people of Cromer really took the matter in hand. They obtained from the Bishop a faculty authorising them to sell four of the five bells, the lead from the roof, "and also such of the timber and board of the said roof that may be saleable". With the money thus obtained they were to put the Church " into such order as that (although it be not restored to its former State) Divine Service may with decency be celebrated therein". Further sums were collected; and the repairs then undertaken, although aesthetically regrettable, tided the Church over into the nineteenth century.

Throughout that century Cromer grew in size and prosperity,

and was a very different place from the parish whose "poor fisher-
men and some few tradesmen" had petitioned the Bishop in 1767.
Rich benefactors and lesser subscribers joined together in a thorough
restoration of the Church; and eventually, more than two hundred
years after its destruction, the chancel was rebuilt—so sympatheti-
cally and harmoniously that many observers do not perceive it to be
a modern piece of work.

REVOLUTIONARY NORWICH

ADMIRERS OF R. H. MOTTRAM's novel *The Boroughmonger*, that
extraordinarily vivid picture of an election campaign at "Easthampton" in the eighteen-thirties, will recall the meeting of the Brethren
of the Cresset, a club of citizens who held democratic and progressive views. Mr Mottram describes the speakers at that meeting,
reproduces their arguments and suggests their widely varying shades
of opinion, with his accustomed historical skill. I do not know if he
had in mind any particular club that may have existed in Norwich
just before the passing of the Reform Bill. But a club did exist there,
forty years or so before the period of his novel, with which some at
least of the Brethren of the Cresset would have been in sympathy;
and I have lately come across an interesting relic of it.

The repercussions of the French Revolution in England are a
familiar story. Like other revolutions, it was welcomed with enthusiasm by many who were to be completely disillusioned by its
later developments. Like other revolutions, again, it passed into a
phase of aggression outside the borders of its own country. Before
long Britain and France were at war; and there took place the historic cleavage within the Whig party, with those who upheld the
views of Burke joining the Government ranks, and Fox remaining at
the head of a depleted Opposition. But the Whig Opposition, for all
its lip-service to democracy, had little genuine contact with the
masses of the people. The humbler sympathisers with the Revolution
expressed their support by forming associations and clubs, and the
London Corresponding Society in particular. The aims of this body
were the holding of meetings and discussions, the issuing of pamphlets
and other propaganda, and sundry long-term objectives such as the

institution of universal suffrage and annual parliaments. On the basis of a weekly subscription of one penny it soon achieved a membership of several thousands, and formed many provincial branches. Perhaps the strongest of these were at Manchester, Sheffield and Norwich.

Not long ago I bought a volume of pamphlets in which someone had inserted a creased and faded document. It was a copy of a letter addressed by the London Corresponding Society, through its secretaries John Ashby and Alexander Galloway, to the branch at Norwich through its secretary John Lightbody of No. 2, Upper Goat Lane. Lightbody had forwarded the copy, with some comments of his own, to a Mr Took, who was in charge of a "division" at Blyford in Suffolk.

The letter is headed "Committee Room, 20th September, 1795", and opens in an exalted and visionary strain:
"Citizens,

We received yours of the 8 Inst. with Pleasure. We congratulate you upon the increase of your Members, and the rapid progress that Knowledge is making in the country. The Sun of Truth is arisen, and sheds its influence on the four Quarters of the Globe. Mankind begins to awake and shake themselves, and like the Roaring of a Lion, the voice of the People is heard, and Tyranny and Oppression begins to Tremble. Reason and Fortitude appear to have superseded Bigotry and pale-eyed Timidity. Ambition, the Soul of War, shall be humbled, and Peace with plenty crown'd shall supersede the hostile Clamours of contending Nations. Yes, fellow Citizens, we look forward with steady and strengthened hopes to the great object of our pursuits, not doubting that our endeavours shall be crown'd with Success. The Miser may as soon be prevail'd upon to give up his Gold, or the Lover to desist from his amorous Pursuits, as those men who are guided by Philanthropy and the Love of Liberty to cease their endeavours in the cause of Reformation. . . ."

The writers then descend to more practical matters. "We fix not our hopes in the present Members of the Opposition, experience having taught us that the moment they shall be placed in Power, Reform will be evaded with the same degree of cunning as it is by those hypocritical deceivers that now steer the course of corruption." Much the same thing is being said today by our journals of the extreme left about the present Government and the present Opposition. "We lament that too many of our Countrymen are still immers'd in that species of Ignorance and Folly that regards splendid Appearance and dignified Titles to constitute the Honour and

Glory of a Nation. But however distant it may be from the present moment, we have every reason to believe that these follies will disappear with the age that hugs them; and that the rising Generation instructed in the Rights of Man, will not suffer themselves to be any longer dup'd by venal Courtiers and delusive Sophists." More than a century and a half has passed, and titles and courtiers are with us still, and the extreme left is still inveighing against them.

The letter concludes with various matters of business. The numbers of the parent Society were continuing to rise, 1800 new members having joined since the last general meeting. They were sending the Norwich branch fifty copies of their report, and other literature later on. And so they remained "with every well wish for the cause of Freedom, yours with Fraternal Affection".

This letter hardly seems a very revolutionary document, but John Lightbody and his branch treated it with some caution. After all Thomas Hardy, the former secretary of the London Corresponding Society, had been arrested and tried for high treason just a year before; and although he was acquitted, it was unwise to take risks. "Citizen Took", wrote Lightbody, "I have sent you a Complete Copy of the Letter we receiv'd from the London Corresponding Society; but we came to a Resolution last Meeting not to copy it at all, but as it was come into the Country I have sent it to you, but I hope you will not let it go out of your hands nor suffer a copy of it to be taken on any Account. Our Numbers increase very fast. Next meeting we shall have 27 Divisions. On the 5th of November we shall celebrate the Acquittal of Citizen Hardy, all the Divisions in Norwich will have a Dinner at their respective Houses. There will be a Public Dinner at the Rose. Any Country friend that can come we shall be glad to see. Pray write to me as soon as you can for I have wrote two Letters to you and have not received any Answer.

I remain your Sincere Fellow Citizen,

John Lightbody."

To this letter Lightbody added some details of a meeting which his branch had held on 6th October. It had been suggested that they should hold an inquiry into the high price of grain; but it was "Resolved not to meddle with it, as the *Loyal Clubs* in this City are going to petition Parliament on that Subject." The Loyal Clubs were composed of their opposite numbers, the citizens who actively supported the Government: but the rise in the cost of living, after almost three years of war, had become a matter of universal concern.

"Appointed a Committee to select from Thelwall's Lectures on the Present Scarcity of Provisions, and to point out a Proper Remedy, viz., a thorough Reform." The report of this committee would be printed, and he would send some copies to Citizen Took. Finally, a note that the stock of the Society amounted to nine pounds.

If Citizens Lightbody and Took were young men they may have lived to rejoice, like the Brethren of the Cresset, at the passing of the Reform Bill—the first step in the direction of universal suffrage, one of the principal ambitions of their Society. It would have seemed to them at least some slight fulfilment of the aspirations of their ardent youth.

THE
NINETEENTH
CENTURY

ROBERT FORBY

NEWCOMERS TO NORFOLK, confronted by an unknown word or an unexpected turn of phrase, often ask whether there exists any glossary of the dialect which still happily survives in these parts; and it is always a pleasure to advise them to obtain a copy of Forby's *Vocabulary of East Anglia*. The two modest volumes, published more than a century ago, have been supplemented but never yet superseded. Modern philologists may smile at some of Forby's derivations, and his *Vocabulary* certainly presents a contrast to the businesslike compilations which embody the results of their learning and research. But the amplitude of Forby's methods, the digressions and speculations and anecdotes in which he constantly indulged, give his book a leisurely charm which is lacking in more recent and more efficient works of etymology.

Robert Forby was born at Stoke Ferry in 1759. He was educated at the free school of King's Lynn and at Caius College, Cambridge, where he became a Fellow, but soon left Cambridge and accepted the living of Horningtoft. In 1799 he became Rector of Fincham, where he remained for the rest of his uneventful life. He gained a considerable reputation as a tutor of private pupils, one of whom was Dawson Turner. He also took part in local administration, and was for many years an active magistrate, although he lamented the "heavy drudgery" which his public work entailed, and described himself sitting down at the end of a long day "with my head full of parish rates, surveyors' accounts, vagrants, runaway husbands, assaults, petty larcenies, militia lists and substitutes, tax duplicates and distress warrants, jumbled together in a horrid confusion". He early adopted the habit of noting down the peculiarities of the Norfolk dialect, and at intervals worked up his notes into what he liked to call his *Icenian Glossary*, to which he added a long introduction and other apparatus. He was never able to put the finishing touches to his book, but it was advancing towards completion when he died suddenly in 1825. It was prepared for the press by the Rev. George Turner of Kettleburgh, and was published in 1830, with an agreeable memoir by his old pupil Dawson Turner.

A great deal can be learnt from Forby's glossary, and from the appendix on popular superstitions and customs, which is one of the most interesting portions of the work. His section on the old East Anglian game of "camping", for example, is full of details which might otherwise have vanished altogether. The pages on witchcraft, on divination, on local proverbs are packed with valuable material. A remarkable number of the words listed by Forby are still current at the present time; but the fluctuations in the use and meaning of some of them, between his day and our own, are very curious. He describes in detail the method of curing a "blown herring", otherwise known as a "tow-blowen", and adds haughtily that "they are also called bloaters, but we do not acknowledge the word". Again, his sole definition of "mardle" is "a pond convenient for watering cattle": and its more familiar use, now made increasingly current by a well-liked contributor to the *Eastern Daily Press,* only appeared in the later supplementary volume by the Rev. W. T. Spurdens.

Forby was sometimes criticised for including a good many words and phrases which do not belong exclusively to East Anglia; but his critics did not reflect that a man who spent his whole life in Norfolk can hardly have known that certain dialect-words, which seemed to him of purely local use, were in fact current all over the English countryside. He was a devoted student of Shakespeare and the Elizabethan dramatists; and his notes often reveal that words and expressions used by Shakespeare in Queen Elizabeth's day, and sufficiently obsolete to puzzle Doctor Johnson and the other great commentators of the eighteenth century, were still in active use in rural Norfolk in the reign of George IV. He loved to smile at the perplexities and wranglings of those learned men, and to observe that a few minutes' talk with one of his own parishioners would have explained to them what Puck meant by a "minnock" and King Lear by a "crow-keeper". But in his note on "harnsey", which means a heron, he himself failed to provide the probable explanation of Hamlet's cryptic saying: "When the wind is southerly, I know a hawk from a handsaw." I believe that some of the most conservative of Shakespearian scholars are now prepared to sanction the reading of "harnsey" for "handsaw". And this view is pleasantly endorsed by the former owner of an annotated copy of Forby now in my possession. In the margin he has transcribed a scrap of excellent Norfolk picked up from a country boy about 1860. "I well remember my father used to read to us out of a right ancient book, how every gentleman in Norfolk rode about with a hawk perked on his wrist, and they used to hawk at them there harnseys and lead 'em a rare life!"

THE LIFE OF COTMAN

THE MEMORY OF JOHN SELL COTMAN is greatly honoured in his native city. Thanks to the generosity of one munificent family, a superb collection of his work has become the permanent possession of Norwich, and may now be seen in one of the new Colman Galleries under ideal conditions. The spacious house which bears his name, so long the scene of his high hopes and frustrated endeavours, has been preserved for a happy and worthy use. Poor Cotman! One wishes that as he stumbled through life, anxious, penurious, unsuccessful as the world reckons success, he could have had some foreknowledge of these things.

I have been reading again the late Sidney D. Kitson's biography of Cotman, which first appeared in 1937. It was the outcome of many years of patient research, and the author died, I think, very soon after its publication. It is an admirable book, sympathetic, scholarly, detailed and accurate. The illustrations are numerous and well reproduced, and cover every aspect of Cotman's extremely varied output. I can imagine no better presentation of the life-story of one of Norfolk's two supreme painters.

I found particular interest, during my re-reading of the book, in the chapters dealing with Cotman's years at Yarmouth as drawing-master in the family of the antiquarian banker Dawson Turner. It was a pleasant relationship. He was able to enjoy, under Turner's firm but kindly handling, a long period of happiness and security. On the other hand he was obliged to fall in with his patron's interests; and so it came about that a landscape-painter of genius spent some of the best years of his life in the production of count-less antiquarian and achitectural drawings. As Mr Kitson pointed out, Turner had no appreciation of Cotman's oil-paintings, and did not include a single one of them in his collection; he might have acquired such pictures as *The Waterfall* for a few pounds, and crammed his Yarmouth house with oil-paintings and water-colours of matchless quality. But he preferred to fill his portfolios and extra-illustrate his Blomefield with meticulous drawings of doorways and fonts and brasses.

Every man is entitled to his own taste, and it would be unjust to blame Dawson Turner for not perceiving the true bent of Cot-man's genius. His general influence on the painter's life was wholly

beneficent; and Cotman's own mind, moreover, had a strongly
antiquarian cast. We may indeed lament with Mr Kitson, as we
turn the pages of *The Sepulchral Brasses of Norfolk*, that "the hands
and brain which had created *The Ploughed Field* and *The Waterfall*" were employed so wastefully on these elaborate reproductions.
All the same, how fortunate we are in Norfolk that the antiquities of
our county, its monasteries and churches and castles and mansions,
should have been depicted by so eminent a hand! Few of us are able
to possess original work by Cotman; our visits to public galleries are
perhaps not very frequent; but Cotman's masterly etchings, and the
engravings after his drawings, have given pleasure to generations of
East Anglians. A copy of *The Architectural Antiquities of Norfolk*,
or even *Excursions through Norfolk* despite its rather too diminutive
plates, will remain a constant delight to the owner.

The penultimate chapter of Mr Kitson's book contains a long and
touching description of Cotman's last visit to Norfolk. The closing
years of his life brought him a modest measure of prosperity. In 1834,
after a long period of failure and despondency in Norwich, he
obtained the Professorship of Drawing at King's College, London;
and since that time he had remained in London almost continuously.
But he still had anxieties about his family, his work, his health; and
he decided in the autumn of 1841 to restore his spirits by a long
holiday in his native county. "He felt", says Mr Kitson, "that the
flame of creative energy, damped down so long by depression and
ill-fortune, was once more alive within him." So he travelled by sea
to Yarmouth and thence by coach to Norwich, visiting Dawson
Turner and other old friends in various parts of Norfolk, and making
a series of sketches which Mr Kitson regarded as "among the most
purposeful studies done direct from Nature which have ever been
produced by a landscape painter".

Much of this holiday was spent in the north of Norfolk, in the
countryside which he had known so well in the days when he was
courting his wife, Ann Miles of Felbrigg, more than thirty years
before. Once again he stood on the cliffs at Cromer, and made a
splendid drawing of a storm far out at sea. He visited Itteringham
and Blickling, Tuttington and Wickmere, Hanworth and Sheringham, at each place sketching groups of trees or some feature in the
church. He called at Wolterton Hall to see a celebrated picture by
Rubens, a landscape with a rainbow: and from the portico of the
Hall he made a drawing of the park, where a sudden shower had
produced a rainbow as glorious as that depicted on Rubens's canvas.

He described the last day of his holiday in a letter to Dawson Turner. "I galloped over Mousehold Heath on that day, for my time was short, through a heavy hail-storm, to dine with my Father—but was obliged to stop and sketch a magnificent scene on the top of the hill leading down to Col. Harvey's house, of trees and gravel pit. But Norfolk is full of such scenes. Oh! rare and beautiful Norfolk."

He returned to London next day, and died there in the following summer without ever revisiting the "rare and beautiful Norfolk" where he is remembered with such admiration and pride.

THE NORWICH MAGAZINE

THE LENGTH OF LIFE enjoyed by newspapers and magazines is subject to great variations. Certain of our present-day newspapers, both national and provincial, can boast a remarkable span of continuous existence. Such periodicals as *Blackwood's* and the *Quarterly Review* stretch back to the earliest years of the nineteenth century. Many other undertakings, now defunct, occupy an honoured place in the history of British journalism. But there have been even more which were launched with the highest hopes and expectations, struggled on for a few years or perhaps only a few issues, and then faded into oblivion.

These failures, like their more successful competitors, have often a very real value for the historian. They play their part in illuminating the vanished scene. They reveal what people were thinking and doing, how the currents of opinion were shifting to and fro, in a particular environment at a particular time. So I was glad to acquire the other day a volume containing the twelve issues of one of these ventures, *The Norwich Magazine*, which ran its brief course during the year 1835. It was printed in monthly parts, by Josiah Fletcher in the Upper Haymarket; and at the end of the year the collected issues were provided with a title-page, an index, and an outspoken preface reviewing its career and indicating the causes of its demise.

The editors, in their opening address, spoke of the discouragements which had at first attended their efforts. Several friends and potential contributors thought the publication of a magazine in Norwich "so forlorn a hope that they declined taxing their leisure and ability to

provide adornments for a castle in the air". Now that it had been
launched, however, those "highly talented individuals" were asked
to give of their best. Contributions of every kind were invited—
poetry, philosophy, "the most interesting branches of physical
science", biography, history, the *belles lettres* in all their forms. Two
topics would be rigorously excluded—sectarian theology and party
politics. "The Wars of the Roses were nobleness itself compared with
the demoralising and debasing Wars of the Ribbons; and we promise
ourselves at least the satisfaction of adding no fuel to that baleful
fire which has consumed so much of the social comfort and moral
respectability of this fair city."

The passing of the Reform Bill, three years before, had enlarged
the franchise without in any way diminishing political strife. In
Norwich the Wars of the Ribbons—the Whig blue and white against
the Tory orange and purple—raged with unabated violence; and
quiet citizens of moderate views, such as one imagines the editors to
have been, were sick and tired of it all. Nevertheless their ban on
politics was not extended to the lectures and debates at the Norwich
Mechanics' Institute, which at times took on a political tinge
although not supposed to do so. Each month they reported the pro-
ceedings of the Institute, whose purpose was "to disperse the clouds
of ignorance before the rising sun of instruction"; and very stimu-
lating some of the discussions must have been.

One evening, for example, the redoubtable Jacob Henry Tillett,
then an ardent reformer aged 17, initiated a debate on the desira-
bility of elections by secret ballot. He was opposed by Miss Jarvis,
who "asserted the greater freedom and nobility of open voting, and
that its abolition would sap the foundations of the British character".
On another occasion Miss Jarvis, "in an extremely beautiful and
eloquent essay", introduced the question: "Is there any moral
obligation to pay taxes?" I wish I knew more about Miss Jarvis. She
seems to have been the only lady who ventured to raise her voice at
the discussions of the Mechanics' Institute, and she raised it very
frequently indeed.

These debates ranged over a wide field. Mr John Copeman
initiated one on the question: "Is it the duty of a free state to provide
for the education of its poor?" In another, the members sought to
determine upon the best man who ever lived, outside sacred history.
The result was a dead heat between Alfred the Great and John
Howard. On another occasion Mr Robert Miller lectured on Elec-
tricity, "to a very numerous audience, which, however, had the

unfortunate effect of so damping his valuable apparatus, as to cause the partial failure of many of his most beautiful experiments".

I do not think the original contributions make quite such good reading, after the lapse of 120 years, as the reports of these debates. Most of them were pseudonymous or unsigned; and although William Taylor was no doubt regarded as the star contributor, his *Lines to the Rainbow* and his *Ode from the German of Klopstock* are not very inspiring productions. Still, the unpretentious little magazine is typical of the better aspects of provincial England in the early nineteenth century—the effort of a kindly, civilised, modestly progressive group of people "to raise the tone of mind and morals in their native city".

Its failure was perhaps equally typical of the less attractive aspects of the age. In their preface to the collected volume the editors really let themselves go. "What, we repeat, are the causes which have combined to crush the rising spirit of inquiry, and render abortive our attempt to provide reading for all? The hour is past when we might shirk this question—the time has come now for speaking out. Norwich is corrupt to her core. The demon of party, like a foul and fearful incubus, has too long been pressing upon her community, and stunting her moral and intellectual growth. . . ." And so forth, at considerable length. They did not actually suggest that the gentle light of *The Norwich Magazine* was deliberately snuffed out by the demon of party. But it might well be contended that party politics remained the chief preoccupation of the citizens of Norwich for many years to come, to the exclusion of more intellectual pursuits. I hope that before long someone will write a full-scale political history of Norwich during the nineteenth century. It should prove a remarkable and at times a startling narrative.

THE EASTERN ARBORETUM

SOME TIME IN THE EIGHTEEN-THIRTIES a young Scotsman named James Grigor set up in business as a nurseryman and "land improver" in Norwich. Partly as a relaxation from business and partly in the course of it, he travelled all over Norfolk, making careful notes upon the parks and gardens, woodlands and specimen trees. Eventually he worked up these notes into a book called *The Eastern Arboretum*, which was issued in fifteen numbers during 1840 and 1841, and was later published as a single volume, with fifty etchings of the most remarkable trees in the county by that excellent artist Henry Ninham. A second edition appeared in 1847, so that it is by no means a scarce book; and I recommend it to anyone interested in trees and in the appearance of the Norfolk countryside a century ago. Its author died in Norwich, still a comparatively young man, in the spring of 1848.

I cannot commend the book as a masterpiece of style. Grigor wrote in the florid and expansive manner beloved of the topographical journalists of his time. "Child of the North—reared amidst storms and hurricanes—the tree of our native country!—we esteem thee above all others. To us thou art fairer than Lebanon's excellency. The olive and the myrtle may scent the eastern evening, but we account thy fragrance sweeter than all. . . ." Thus, as a good Scotsman, he apostrophised the Scots Pine; and there is much in the same vein in every chapter. His excursions into history are wildly unreliable; he might have been expected to say, as he does, that Anne Boleyn was born at the earlier Blickling Hall, but it is startling to learn that it was also "the occasional resort of William the Conqueror". These are the faults of the book; but it has many merits. Grigor did not confine his investigations to the great estates, but described with equal care the best trees in scores of little properties all over the county; he paid the same scrupulous attention to the ilexes at Holkham and the hawthorns in the garden of Mrs Colonel Diggins at East Dereham. His work, moreover, was based on great technical experience. He knew an immense amount about trees and their culture; on questions of species, soil, climate, planting, pruning, thinning, his views were very sound. And he loved trees as well as he understood them; his passion for his subject shines through every pompous adjective and every turgid sentence.

More than a hundred years after Grigor toured the Norfolk countryside, some of the trees which he admired are still identifiable —the group of chestnuts near Hevingham Church; the spreading plane in the garden at Blickling; the cedar of Lebanon at Stratton Strawless; the roadside oak near Wymondham popularly associated with Kett. I believe that portions still remain of two of the most venerable trees depicted by Ninham, the Winfarthing oak and the Hethel thorn; and the third of these "vegetable wonders of Norfolk", the colossal oak at Thorpe Market, continues to flourish, and must surely be the finest tree now existing in the county.

In Grigor's day, the planting of hardwoods for shipbuilding was still extensively carried on, and the afforestation of large areas with softwood trees was not yet the rule. Some types of conifer, now planted for timber, were recent introductions carefully tended in park or pleasure ground; it was not yet realised that they are perfectly hardy in the English climate. For instance, the tree known as the "monkey puzzle", which withstands our hardest frosts only too well, was then an exciting novelty. Ninham portrayed a young specimen at Wolterton, a scaly little horror in striking contrast to the magnificent beech which he drew on the same estate; and Grigor observed, almost with awe, that "it rises to the height of nine feet nine inches, and bears the rigour of winter with a very slight protection".

Grigor was a student of Humphry Repton's writings, and an admirer of his achievements as a landscape gardener; and he loved to discourse, in the Reptonian manner, on the general appearance and particular amenities of the estates which he visited. Usually he found much to praise and little to blame; but it can hardly have pleased one landowner to be told that his trees were so drawn up for lack of thinning that they could only be used for scaffold poles, another that his lodge gates had a "prim and unparklike effect only suited to a suburban villa", and a third that his property was so neglected that the owl and the bittern would soon possess it.

As for Norwich, Grigor seems to have known every tree and shrub within his adopted city. He advocated the laying-out of a fine public garden there, something better than Chapel Field, which "from its being so much the resort of loose and idle boys, and being occupied partly by washerwomen, seems to be in a great measure deserted by the respectable citizens". He longed to see "the barren frontiers of Mousehold" covered with flourishing woods. But these were visionary schemes; and he turned from them to record the elms and limes, the planes and poplars, the mulberries, walnuts, willows, acacias, maples, medlars and laburnums which "give our city all the character of a country village". In the same way he took his readers through the suburbs and surrounding villages—Thorpe, which he called "the Richmond of Norfolk", Catton, Heigham, Lakenham, Eaton, with all their sequestered gardens, their tranquil lawns, their ancient trees. It is probable that Norfolk—and, indeed, all England —never looked more beautiful than during the years when Grigor was writing his book. The creations of the planters and landscape artists of the previous century were reaching their full maturity. Architecture had not yet entered upon its grim Victorian decline. And the first railway tentacles, those heralds of progress and prosperity and gloom and grime, were only just beginning to spread into the East Anglian countryside.

SPANNING THE
CENTURIES

THE VANISHED HEYDONS

A FEW WEEKS AGO I was putting together some notes about the Heydon family, and went once more to look at the remains of the great houses which they built at Baconsthorpe and Saxlingham in the days of their splendour. It was a perfect summer afternoon, with the cornfields, some of them almost ready for harvest, contrasting most beautifully with the deep green of the woods; and although the sun blazed steadily down, and the long July drought showed no sign of breaking, a cool wind was blowing in from the sea. Characteristic sounds of the twentieth century, the droning of aircraft and the familiar gunfire along the coast, broke at times into the stillness: but as soon as they were silent the whole countryside returned to its drowsy peace, and it was again possible to meditate on the Heydons and their strange vicissitudes of fortune.

The Heydons resembled another Norfolk family, the Pastons, in their meridian grandeur and their sudden decline. One may compare the first Sir Christopher Heydon in the sixteenth century, entertaining to a Christmas dinner at Baconsthorpe the thirty master shepherds of his widespread flocks, with the contemporary Pastons and the state they kept at Paston and Oxnead. Then, in both families, came personal extravagance, unsuccessful speculation, a fondness for such unpractical and often expensive pursuits as astrology and alchemy, and their gallant but unavailing support of the royal cause in the Civil War. The fortunes of Sir John Heydon, that gay and valiant soldier, with his taste for easy badinage and his love of abstruse learning, had virtually foundered even before the war began; and by the close of the seventeenth century the male line of the family was extinct, and Baconsthorpe already a ruin. The Pastons held on for a generation or two longer, and if the Stuart rule had continued they might once again have been powers in the land; but they soon faded from view in the unsympathetic climate of Hanoverian England.

The ruins at Baconsthorpe are in the care of the Ministry of Works, and substantial repairs to them are now being undertaken. The size and scale of that "spacious, sumptuous pile", which Sir Henry Heydon is recorded to have "built entirely from the ground, except the tower (which was built by his father) in the space of six years", can once again be properly appreciated. The ruins have been so despoiled in the past that their interest is perhaps architectural rather than visual, although the gatehouse still retains one of the sixteenth-century turrets which figure in the engraving after Humphry Repton, and the fine barn stands much as it must have done in the time of the Heydons, though with very different machinery within. All around lie the quiet fields, where once the existence of a great Tudor household, with its bustle and hospitality and incessant comings and goings, made Baconsthorpe the centre of this whole countryside.

In the middle of the village stands the church, also with its memories of the Heydons—effigies and inscriptions in brass, armorial stained glass of excellent quality in many of the windows, and the fine monument to Sir William Heydon at the end of the south aisle. It is said that Sir William, "by engaging in several projects with certain citizens of London, contracted a large debt, and sold much of his paternal estate", and thus began the downfall of his family; but on his memorial he appears in high dignity as a faithful servant of his country and county, on sea and land, in war and in peace.

The house at Saxlingham, which stood in a field close to the church, was built by the first Sir John Heydon, son of the builder of Baconsthorpe. The porch still remains intact, with three armorial tablets of well-carved stone set in the flintwork. Everything else is a confusion of crumbling farm-buildings and broken walls, thickly overgrown with ivy. It must have been a noble mansion; it was apparently still in fair order in the eighteenth century, with the matches of the Heydons in stained glass in the windows of the great parlour, and "on the top of the house a place to take a view of the country". It was a favourite residence of the second Sir Christopher Heydon, the son of Sir William, under whom the family fortunes declined still further. Sir Christopher was passionately addicted to astrology, and gave full rein to his astrological and hieroglyphic fantasies in the monument to the memory of his first wife in Saxlingham Church—a riot of allegory and symbolism, briefly described in the essay which follows.

BACONSTHORPE CASTLE

THE ANCIENT HOME of the Heydons at Baconsthorpe is not easy to find. Even the handsome new sign-posts of the Ministry of Works cannot direct the visitor infallibly through the wandering roads of north Norfolk. But when he reaches his destination, his journey will be well rewarded. Year by year the Ministry's employees have been clearing away the mantle of ivy and undergrowth which hid the details and almost the very outlines of the ruins. They have removed the trees whose roots were splitting the walls asunder. They have restored the full width of the moat all round the enclosure. The superb quality of the flintwork of the great gatehouse is fully revealed. There is still much to be done; but everywhere the grey walls stand clear and unencumbered, set off by the foliage of horse-chestnut and sycamore and beech.

The scale of the buildings bears impressive witness to the power and opulence of the Heydons in their prime. But their splendour was short-lived. Baconsthorpe seems to have been completed about the time of the accession of King Henry VII, and the fortunes of the family reached their zenith under the great Sir Christopher in the reign of the first Queen Elizabeth. While she was still on the throne, their decline had begun. Sir Christopher's son and his successors were brave soldiers and high-spirited gentlemen, hot-tempered duellists when occasion arose, but increasingly extravagant and unpractical in the management of their affairs. The cult of astrology, with all its elaborate mystical nonsense, held an intense fascination for them. They were deep in debt even before Sir John Heydon, Lieutenant-General of the Ordnance to King Charles I during the Civil War, lost the remains of his estate through his steadfast adherence to the royal cause.

Blomefield tells us that "the chief part of this hall was pulled down in 1650". I have found an interesting confirmation of this in an account-book of 1654. During that year John Windham of Felbrigg made substantial purchases of stone from Baconsthorpe, no doubt from the recently demolished portions of the building. In June his steward paid half a crown to a mason called Henry Natt for "one day measuringe stone at Bacconsthorpe", and two shillings for the expenses there of three other men. A week later he paid six shillings "ffor Beere at Baconsthorp for the Carters belonging to 18 Cartes", and a further shilling for beer to three more carters. In August eleven carters received payments for bringing stone to Felbrigg, and for the inevitable beer. The actual payments for the stone were made to one John Cressy, if I have read the name correctly—£25 in November, and £10 more in the following March.

I do not know for what purpose John Windham required this large consignment of stone. No new building or extensive repair was being undertaken at Felbrigg Hall itself at that period. There are entries in the account-books of repairs to various farm-buildings, but I have come across nothing that suggests the use of a quantity of stone specially carted from some distance away. No doubt others besides Windham were equally ready to avail themselves of the material from Baconsthorpe; and it is remarkable that the surviving remains, after the lapse of three hundred years, are still so considerable.

I have heard it suggested that Baconsthorpe was besieged and battered down by the Roundhead forces during the Civil War. There is not the slightest evidence, so far as I know, that anything of the sort occurred. Its owner, Sir John Heydon, was absent in the King's service throughout the war; and his property, isolated in this Parliamentarian countryside, was placed under sequestration by the local committee on which his Puritan neighbours, Hobarts and Palgraves and Windhams, so readily served. Baconsthorpe may indeed have begun to fall into decay even before the war began: for quite early in the seventeenth century the Heydons seem to have deserted it in favour of their other house at Saxlingham, a few miles away. It was at Saxlingham that the last Sir Christopher lived, scribbling astrological pamphlets with such titles as *A Recitall of the Caelestiall Apparitions of this present Trygon now in being*, and assisted in their composition by his chaplain William Bredon, who used to smoke the bell-ropes of his church instead of tobacco.

It was in Saxlingham Church also that this Sir Christopher erected to the memory of his first wife Mirabel Rivett an extraordinary monument which filled the entire chancel, so that there was hardly room to walk round it. Tom Martin's drawing of this object has fortunately survived, and supplements the description given by Blomefield. It shows a great square base surrounded by kneeling effigies, and upon it a lofty pyramid tapering to the roof and surmounted by a flaming urn. The surface of the pyramid was composed of panels filled with emblems and astrological hieroglyphics— a hare, a leopard, a child blowing bubbles, a pilgrim, a thunderbolt, "a quiver full of arrows hanging on a lawrell branch", a trumpet encircled by a vine, "the wind blowing on a cock's tail". The whole fantastic structure was swept away in a nineteenth-century restoration. Nothing now remains of this portentous symbol of the Heydons in their extravagant decline, except one little kneeling figure of a child.

SOME PASTON FOOTNOTES

THE PASTON EXHIBITION at Norwich Castle Museum in 1953 greatly revived local interest in that remarkable family. The story of the gradual rise of the Pastons, their long-continued prosperity and sudden decline was most ingeniously expounded in the Museum galleries by means of pictures, furniture, genealogical tables, personal relics and contemporary objects, in fact a multitude of small but significant details. Through the kindness of the Rector of Oxnead, I have since been able to examine the register of that parish, where for two centuries the Pastons had their principal residence; and I can now append a few additional and very minor notes to the story of their fortunes. Incidentally the register, a small square volume, was lost for many years and finally came into the safe hands of the Norfolk antiquary Robert Fitch, who restored it to the parish with an admonitory inscription inside the front cover.

The entries begin in 1573, and one of the earliest is a record of the burial on 26th December 1589 of *Margeria Paston, generosa*. It is difficult to be certain, but I suspect that this gentlewoman must have been the Margery Paston who was once a nun at the great convent of Barking in Essex. When Barking suffered the fate of all religious houses in the reign of Henry VIII, the nuns were dismissed with pensions; and Margery Paston is known to have been allotted a pension of eight marks a year, and to have returned home to her family in Norfolk. It is strange to think of her living on at Oxnead, bearing her memories of choir and cloister into a world so utterly changed, and witnessing in extreme old age the alarm and exultation of the Armada year.

The mansion at Oxnead had been built during the sixteenth century by Clement Paston, the second son of the first Sir William Paston

and a brother of Margery the nun. Clement Paston had fought with
distinction both on sea and land, and was the trusted servant of four
of the Tudor monarchs, two kings and two queens. In his old age
he retired to Oxnead and lived there, in Fuller's words, "honourably,
quietly and in good housekeeping". His wife, who is depicted kneeling at the side of his monument in Oxnead Church, had been pre-
viously married to a certain Richard Lambert of London; and as
there was no issue of her second marriage, the "good housekeeping"
at Oxnead was shared in a generous measure by her son Edmund
Lambert and his numerous progeny. The registers contain several
entries relating to this family—Giles Lambert marries Elizabeth
Reimes, Roger Mountney marries Elizabeth Lambert, and so forth.
Clement Paston died in 1597. After his death his widow and stepson
continued to live at Oxnead, and died within a month of one
another twelve years later. They were buried under fine stone slabs,
with inscriptions and armorials in brass, before the altar in Oxnead
Church.

Twenty years later, in the decade before the Civil War, the third
Sir William Paston made Oxnead for a short time the most famous
house in Norfolk, renowned for its collections of works of art, the
elaborate beauty of its gardens, and its open-handed hospitality. The
registers record the births of his children, and the death of his first
wife Lady Katherine, whose monument by Nicholas Stone, with its
exquisite portrait-bust, is still to be seen in the church. Then came
the Civil War and Sir William's attempts in support of the King,
followed by the heavy fines which impoverished him for life and
permanently crippled the family estate.

The entries in the register during the latter half of the seventeenth
century are strangely casual and disconnected. They are sympto-
matic, in their humble way, of the growing insecurity which under-
lay the magnificence of the Pastons during the reigns of the later
Stuarts. When Sir Robert Paston, first Earl of Yarmouth, Lord-
Lieutenant of Norfolk, High Steward of Great Yarmouth, died in
1683, his obsequies were splendidly conducted at Oxnead, and the
walls of the little church resounded to a funeral sermon of sonorous
eulogy; but no monument was erected to his memory, and no entry
of his burial was even made in the register. It was the same with all
his sons and grandsons, the last of all their line. In the intimate
records of their own parish, it is as though they had never been.

This sense of doom, of the approaching extinction of a great family,
seems to me to be suggested yet again, and most unexpectedly,

in the extraordinary painting called *The Yarmouth Collection*, which hangs in Strangers' Hall. Here are heaped together in wild profusion the objects in which the hearts of the later Pastons delighted—cups and tankards richly embossed, goblets of agate and crystal, splendid hangings, instruments of music, all sorts of treasures. But in one corner the painter has also depicted a candle guttering towards its end, an hour-glass with its sands fast running away, a clock with its hands at half past eleven. This is surely a group of deliberate references to the transitory nature of all earthly splendour. For Lord Yarmouth and his family, as they struggled to maintain their ascendancy in Norfolk in the treacherous reign of Charles II, such symbols must have held a meaning of which they were all too well aware.

THE PASTON MEMORIALS

TWO CENTURIES HAVE GONE by since the Pastons vanished from their ancient homes in Norfolk. But, more than most extinguished families, they have left their memorials behind them. The letters which record their early struggles in the fifteenth century provide a matchless source of historical and personal information about that turbulent age. The Grammar School at North Walsham, which Sir William Paston founded early in the reign of James I, flourishes greatly and in every way fulfils his high intentions. And the most tangible memorials of the family, their monuments of stone and marble and alabaster, still adorn the churches in which they used to worship.

Two of these stand in the little church of Oxnead. On the north side of the sanctuary is the fine alabaster tomb of Clement Paston, the builder of Oxnead Hall, a distinguished soldier and sailor, the trusted servant of two kings and two queens. His effigy in armour is recumbent upon the tomb-chest, and a smaller figure of his widow kneels beside it. Close by, and some thirty years later in date, is Lady Katherine Paston's beautiful memorial in black and white marble, the work of Nicholas Stone. Both these monuments had suffered grievous damage from time and accident; and in 1956 the Pilgrim Trust made a generous grant for their repair. This was admirably carried out under the supervision of the late Mr S. J. Wearing.

I would like to place on record in these columns two small points connected with the Oxnead monuments. When examining Clement Paston's tomb lately, I noticed an inscription cut rather roughly along the upper edge of the right-hand shield on the tomb-chest. This reads: "REP. WILLIAM BRIGST. 1660" (or perhaps 1665 or 1669). The name must be that of William Brigstowe, who is mentioned in one of Sir Thomas Browne's notes as being "mason at the reparation of the steeple" of Norwich Cathedral in 1663, and as having measured the height of the spire in that year. Evidently the Pastons, in the prosperous decade which followed the Restoration, had their ancestor's tomb repaired by the best hand available; but it is odd that Brigstowe was allowed to append his signature in so crude a fashion.

Lady Katherine Paston's monument, with its sensitive portrait-bust of the young wife whom it commemorates, is one of Nicholas Stone's outstanding works, comparable with his lovely effigy of Mrs Coke at Bramfield in Suffolk. The authorship of the poem beginning "Needs she another monument of stone", inscribed on one of the marble tablets which flank the main composition, does not appear to have been traced. It was in fact written by Ralph Knevet, the Pastons' private chaplain at this time, whose masque *Rhodon and Iris*, performed at the Florists' Feast at Norwich in 1631, I described in a previous article. Knevet's only other published work was a volume of *Funerall Elegies, Consecrated to the immortall memory of the Right Honorable the Lady Katherine Paston*. In this he portrays at portentous length, but with a wealth of genuine feeling, the grief at the loss of this gracious lady which was universally felt

> *On that faire tract, where Bure creeps lazily*
> *To pay his tribute to a greater flood.*

I lately examined a copy of this book, perhaps the only copy now surviving; and at the conclusion of the elegies I found the short and touching poem which is carved upon the monument.

The tomb of the founder of the Paston Grammar School stands in the sanctuary of North Walsham Church. In February 1608, Sir William Paston commissioned John Key, citizen and freemason of London, to construct for him a tomb of exceptional magnificence. Every detail was to be carried out to his own long-pondered designs, and in accordance with a most elaborate contract, which has fortunately survived. The central feature was to be "the picture of a man in Armor restinge upon his Arme of five foote and a halfe longe in

Allablaster". The secondary adornments—"Parramidies, Pillers, Epitates, Writtings and Armes"—were likewise specified in detail; and arrangements were made for all contingencies, down to the diet of the masons who were to erect it. The work was completed by the autumn; and Sir William was able to contemplate his own effigy, on his visits to North Walsham, for two years before his death.

On 1st October 1956 the School celebrated the 350th anniversary of its foundation. To mark this event, the Old Pastonian Society defrayed the cost of the expert cleaning of the monument past which its members filed, during their own schooldays, on the morning of each Founder's Day. The work was executed in the careful and conservative manner invariably practised by a noted Cambridge firm. The original gilding and colour, obscured by the dust of so many years, now shine and glow once more with their pristine lustre. Even more beautiful are the natural tones of the splendid alabaster from which so much of the monument is carved. The present appearance of this admirable work of Renaissance sculpture must have amply rewarded the piety of those who undertook its renovation.

NORFOLK AND THE LAW

THE SUPPOSED FONDNESS of Norfolk people for going to law was a standing joke against them in former centuries. I have no means of judging, from the modest sphere of a local Magistrates' Court, how the advocates, the litigants and the defendants of modern Norfolk compare with those of other counties. But in the earlier days our forebears certainly enjoyed a nation-wide reputation for their skill and persistence in legal matters, and for their eagerness to invoke the resources of the law on every possible occasion.

I am not certain how far back in our history this reputation began to develop. The thirteenth-century Latin poem by a monk of Peterborough, in which the wickedness of Norfolk was wrathfully denounced, called us

> *gens vilissima,*
> *Plena versutiis, fallax et invida,*
> *Et nationibus cunctis contraria . . .*

a most worthless race, full of cunning, false and jealous, and (as the

Norfolk people themselves would perhaps have said) "awkward towards all foreigners"; but I do not think the sin of litigiousness is specifically imputed to us anywhere in the poem. Chaucer's reeve in the *Canterbury Tales* was from our county—

> *Of Northfolk was this reve, of which I telle,*
> *Bisyde a toun men clepen Baldeswelle—*

and although he is presented as an extremely good man of business, there is again no suggestion that he displayed any abnormal skill in law.

By the middle of the fifteenth century, however, Norfolk and Norwich had grown so fond of litigation that in 1455 a statute was passed drastically limiting the number of attorneys practising in the county and city. This statute was specially aimed against a certain type of lawyer, "which come to every fair, market, and other places, where any assembly of people is, exhorting, procuring, moving and exciting the people to attempt untrue and foreign suits for small trespasses, little offences, and small sums of debt . . . whereby proceed many suits, more of evil will and malice than of truth of the thing".

The sixteenth and seventeenth centuries produced a galaxy of most eminent Norfolk lawyers, and it was in those centuries that the legal talents of our forebears really became proverbial. In Camden's view—to quote Bishop Gibson's translation of his Latin—"the inhabitants are of a bright clear complexion; not to mention their sharpness of wit, and admirable quickness in the study of our Common-law. So that it is at present, and always has been reputed, the most fruitful Nursery of Lawyers; and even among the common people you shall meet with many who (as one expresses it) if they have no just quarrel, are able to raise it out of the very quirks and niceties of the Law." According to Norden, "they are so well skilled in matters of the Law as many times even the baser Sort at the Plough-tail will argue *pro et contra* cases in Law". "They will enter an action for their neighbour's horse but looking over their hedge", wrote Fuller. "They are good cleare witts, subtile, and the most litigious of England: they carry Littleton's Tenures at the plough taile", was the verdict of Aubrey. "Norfolk wiles many a man beguiles" was a proverb in everybody's mouth, of which Grose also records a more elaborate version: "Essex stiles, Kentish miles, Norfolk wiles, many a man beguiles."

Our Elizabethan and Jacobean lawyers indeed presented an

impressive spectacle. Their Norfolk fellow-countrymen regarded with pride and awe the high places which they held in the councils of the nation, and the worldly splendour which was the reward of their wisdom and eloquence. They have passed into history—Sir Nicholas Bacon, who bought the Stiffkey estate for his second son and embarked upon the building of that stately house; his son-in-law, Judge Francis Windham, whose monument is in St Peter Mancroft and whose picture hangs in the Guildhall at Norwich; Sir Henry Hobart, to whom we owe the tranquil loveliness of Blickling, where a superb portrait of him may still be seen; and above all Sir Edward Coke, with his rich manors scattered all over England, and his writings, which formed the grammar of the humblest student of the law.

Towards the close of the seventeenth century, Norfolk litigiousness appears to have become a stock playwright's joke. Several references of this kind are introduced into Wycherley's *Plain Dealer*, first acted in 1674, in which the principal comic characters are the Widow Blackacre, "a petulant, litigious Widow, always in Law", and her son Jerry, "a true raw Squire, under age and his Mother's government, brèd to the Law". The Widow Blackacre is said by another character to be "as vexatious as a dozen Norfolk attorneys, and as implacable as a wife suing for her alimony, or a parson for his tithes ... when she is in town, she lodges in one of the Inns of Chancery, where she breeds her son, and is his tutoress in law-French; and for her country abode, though she has no estate there, she chooses Norfolk". Later in the play she herself says that "if I would have married a young man, 'tis known I could have had any young heir in Norfolk, nay, the hopefullest young man this day at the King's Bench bar". Quite clearly the conjunction of Norfolk and the law was expected automatically to raise a laugh in the playhouses under King Charles II.

In the eighteenth century the joke seems at last to have petered out; at least I can recall no further references to it. The great figures of the Norfolk scene in that era were politicians rather than lawyers —Sir Robert Walpole and his brother Horatio, the second Lord Townshend and his grandsons George and Charles, William Windham, Thomas William Coke. There have been distinguished lawyers from this county in every century and up to the present moment; but it was in the days of Queen Elizabeth and King James that Norfolk men followed most successfully what the greatest of them described as "the gladsome light of Jurisprudence".

THE GREEN YARD

OUR SEVENTEENTH-CENTURY FOREBEARS enjoyed few things more than a good long sermon. Samuel Pepys, not a particularly devout character, used to listen to them twice a Sunday with critical appreciation—"Mr Mills made a most excellent sermon"; "we had a dull sermon of a stranger which made me sleep"; "a most tedious, unreasonable and impertinent sermon by an Irish Doctor". Beside every pulpit stood an hour-glass. As the sands ran out, a loud hum of approbation would often rise from the packed congregation; and the preacher would then be encouraged to turn the glass upside-down, and embark with undiminished fervour upon a second hour of discourse.

Sermons were not necessarily preached in churches. In London the open-air sermons at St Paul's Cross drew throngs of eager auditors, generation after generation. The Norwich equivalent of St Paul's Cross was the pulpit in the Green Yard, an open space on the north side of the Cathedral. In studying Norwich history one often comes upon references to the Green Yard and the sermons which were preached there. Until the disturbances of the Civil War it played a regular part in the life of the city; and quite possibly someone has already drawn up and published an account of its history. If so, I am afraid I have overlooked it.

The Green Yard was known as "the preechyng yard", and contained a pulpit, as early as 1437. Thanks to Sir Thomas Browne we know a good deal about its appearance and the arrangements for the public sermons there, early in the seventeenth century. By then the pulpit was raised on eight or ten steps of stone; it was covered with lead and surmounted by a leaden cross. Seats had been built against the wall of the Bishop's Palace for the Mayor and aldermen, "so that they were not offended by rayne". The Bishop and his Chancellor used to listen to the sermons at one of the Palace windows. Against the north wall of the Cathedral "places were built gallerywise one above another, where the Deane, Prebends and their wives, gentlemen and the better sort very well heard the sermon". Less important people could sit on forms in the yard itself, paying a penny or halfpenny for their places. The "Hospitall boyes" and others stood on the steps of the pulpit.

In 1617 the Green Yard was the scene of the historic row between

John Mingay, the Mayor of Norwich, and Sir Augustine Palgrave, the High Sheriff of Norfolk, who officiously caused the visiting Lord Chief Justice to place himself in the seat which belonged by ancient right to the Mayor. Although the Mayor "very discreetly and stoutly challenged it to be his seat", his remonstrances had no effect. But next day he was able to prove his case; "upon which the Judges, coming out of their lodgings into their chamber of audience, sat down, and ordered the Mayor to sit down by them, and the High Sheriff standing bare-headed before them, the Lord Chief Justice reprimanded him for his untrue information touching the seat". It was a signal victory for the city over the county, and one whose effects survive in certain forms of precedence to this day.

During the outburst of iconoclasm in Norwich early in the Civil War, the Green Yard was not spared. Bishop Hall tells us that the leaden cross over the pulpit was sawn down and flung into a great bonfire in the market place, together with the organ-pipes and vestments from the Cathedral. The pulpit remained a little longer. In fact the indomitable Bishop, shut out of his own Cathedral, preached from it on the Whitsunday of 1644 to the faithful remnant of his flock. But soon afterwards, according to Browne, it was "taken downe and placed in Newhall Green, which had been the Artillery Yard, and the publick sermon was there preached". I do not think it was brought back at the Restoration, or that the Green Yard was ever used for sermons again.

The seats and galleries were also removed, and before long the Green Yard became a waste space and something of an eyesore. Dean Prideaux's unpublished diary tells us that it lay quite open, so that anyone could walk right under the windows of the Palace; and those windows, and the windows of the Cathedral, were often damaged by the schoolboys playing there and throwing stones. Bishop Trimnell remedied this in 1708 by taking a lease of the Green Yard from the Chapter, and incorporating the area in the grounds of the Palace.

There had always been a doorway out of the Cathedral into the Green Yard, through which a right-of-way, after passing through or across the nave, led to the Palace. Its position is clearly indicated on the ground-plan of the Cathedral in Blomefield's *Norfolk*. Complaints had long been made of the "scandalous but common practise of carrying burthens through it, even during the performance of service"; and Bishop Gooch, soon after his arrival in 1738, decided that this must stop. He made a new approach to the Palace from the

Upper Close, and blocked up the doorway. So vanished the last relic of the Green Yard; but the arch of the doorway is still visible in the outer wall of the nave, under the seventh window from the west end of the Cathedral.

HISTORY FROM THE MONUMENTS

AN EMINENT HISTORIAN, long since dead, once described to me the feelings of excitement and anticipation with which he always entered an English parish church. He could be almost certain, he said, of making some discovery which bore upon his chosen field of study; of lighting upon some architectural or monumental feature which contributed, in however humble a manner, towards his knowledge of the past history of England. He was thinking, in particular, of the memorials—the brasses, the altar-tombs, the mural tablets, the floor-slabs—which almost every parish church contains; and it is indeed from these monuments, with their varied beauty of design and workmanship, that the student of history will derive most instruction and delight.

Some famous Norfolk examples come at once to mind—the Braunche and Walsoken brasses at King's Lynn, with their revelation of the civic magnificence of the fourteenth century; the brass at Felbrigg of Sir Simon Felbrigg and his Czech wife, cousin and *domicella* of Richard II's Queen Anne of Bohemia, with its vivid suggestions, in costume and heraldry, of that sumptuous and cultivated court; the noble works of Nicholas Stone, perhaps the greatest of seventeenth-century statuaries, at Paston and Oxnead, Tittleshall and Holkham. But there are countless memorials of a less spectacular kind, unmentioned in the guide-books, which also make their little contribution to history, and throw a sudden ray of light upon some otherwise forgotten life.

Nothing would be remembered, for example, about Sir Thomas Rant were it not for the beautifully lettered mural tablet which commemorates him in Thorpe Market Church. But his memorial brings him clearly before us—sagacious, conciliatory, steering a prudent course through the difficult times in which he lived. He was a prosperous London lawyer until "his Sovereigne Charles the first was driven from London by the tumults, when retireing into his Native Countrey he lived hospitably and honourably, spending his time successfully in composeing differences and preventing Suites between his Neighbours". When the Commonwealth drew to an end, "he was chosen a Member of the Healing Parliament"—a delightful name for the assembly more usually and prosaically known as the Convention Parliament of 1660, which restored the monarchy, and in which Rant was one of the representatives for Norwich. He was knighted by Charles II, "when a second tyme retireing from the inviteing preferments of his restored King and revived Countrey he privately served God, his Countrey and friends", dying in 1671 generally lamented, "after he had built an Almeshouse and added to the Revenue of the Church".

Sir Thomas Adams is another forgotten figure of the seventeenth century whose career is recorded for us on his monument, in this case a colossal affair in the chancel of Sprowston Church, with fine recumbent effigies of himself and his wife. His Latin epitaph recounts the facts of an eventful life, the high civic offices he held in London, his imprisonment for loyalty to the King, his charity and beneficence; even the medical details, described by a shocked ecclesiologist of the early nineteenth century as "a long and minutely indelicate catalogue of Sir Thomas's ailments", increase our sympathetic interest in this man of three hundred years ago. His younger contemporary, Sir Joseph Paine, who was Mayor of Norwich in the Restoration year and was knighted by Charles II, is brought to mind in a different manner by his monument in St Gregory's Church. Here the inscription has become almost wholly illegible; but Sir Joseph's great pride was his position as "Collonel of the Train'd Bands of the City of Norwich", and his military enthusiasm is still recorded for posterity by the martial emblems beautifully carved upon the monument—sword and helmet, corselet and gauntlets and spurs, flags and trumpets and drum, and a cannon with its full equipment of cannon-balls and powder-barrels and shovel and rammer.

Turning from this warlike array to the arts of peace, we may see in Kimberley Church the fine slab commemorating the famous musician John Jenkins, who passed most of his eighty-six years as an honoured instructor and guest in the country houses of East Anglia. "He was a person of much easier temper than most of his faculty," according to Roger North, "and had a very good sort of wit, which served him in his address and conversation, wherein he did not please less than in his compositions. And his way took with the age he lived in, which was a great happiness to him, but he lived so long that he saw himself outrun and antiquated." Antiquated his music may have seemed in the age of Purcell; but the Wodehouses took care of him at Kimberley to the end of his long life, and buried him under the affectionate rhyming epitaph which we may read today.

And occasionally we may come upon monuments which remind us that Norfolk men played their part in the great overseas enterprises, military and commercial, of earlier centuries. One such memorial is in Wickmere Church; a mural tablet to Henry Spelman, who, "having distinguished himself by his Intrepidity and Conduct as a Soldier at Dettingen and Fontenoy, died at Calcutta in the Kingdom of Bengal the 18 of April, 1765, being then Captain Commandant of the Honble. East India Company's Cavalry there". The inscription goes on to tell posterity that the standard "under which he has often bravely fought" was brought back to England by his friends Peter Downes and Stephen Hoare, and was placed by them in his parish church "in grateful remembrance of his Merit and Friendship". And there, above the monument, the shaft of his standard still remains—twelve feet of stout bamboo, with a few threads of the fabric still adhering to it—as his friends set it up nearly two hundred years ago.

SALTHOUSE AND THE SEA

"NO COUNTY IN ENGLAND doth carry a top and top gallant more high in maritime performances than Norfolk." I was lately reminded of Thomas Fuller's saying by some extracts from the old parish registers of the coastal village of Salthouse. The registers themselves met with disaster during the last war, not through enemy action, but owing to certain injudicious though well-intentioned steps which were taken to ensure their safety. By good fortune a former resident of Salthouse had copied a number of the more interesting entries, and had assembled other valuable details of the history of the parish; and these came into my possession after his death.

The sea was in the blood of the people of Salthouse, and to generation after generation its call was strong. On the benches and desks in the chancel of the Church, schoolboys of the early seventeenth century carved pictures, which still survive, of the ships in which they hoped one day to serve; and when they were a little older, in just such ships they would sail—in coastal traffic along the English seaboard, in trading voyages to the Baltic and the Mediterranean, and on occasion in battle against the enemies of the King.

The voyages, the adventures, the varying fates of the seamen from Salthouse have passed into oblivion; the registers of a parish only chronicle the lives of those who remain at home. But in 1643 there is an entry which reminds us that during a few tragic years, three centuries ago, Englishmen were fighting their fellow-countrymen across our countryside and around our coasts.

"Memorandum that Thomas Bredcocke son of Thomas Bredcocke of Salthouse being slaine in Winterton roade in the Parliament service in a shippe called the Hopefull Luke upon the 30th of August 1643, being Wednesday, was buried in Great Yarmouth Churchyard the 31st of the same being Thursday.

Ita testatur Edw. Dawnay rector ecclesiæ de Salthouse."

Nothing seems to be known about the action in which Thomas Bredcocke lost his life; but it took place during the weeks when the town of King's Lynn, which had declared for the King, was under siege from the Parliamentarian forces. The Royalists in Lynn were constantly expecting ammunition and supplies to reach them by sea, and one ship did succeed in getting through the blockade by giving false signals. I suggest, therefore, that the *Hopefull Luke* may have been stationed off Yarmouth in order to intercept attempts on the part of the Royalists in Holland, where their ships were based, to bring supplies or reinforcements to their hard-pressed comrades in Lynn.

On 22nd November 1625, the register recorded the baptism of one of Norfolk's greatest seamen, Sir Christopher Myngs. His parents— "John Myngs of ye parish of St. Katherines in ye Cittye of London and Katherine Parre"—had been married in Salthouse Church two years before. Mrs Myngs's father owned property in Salthouse and Kelling, and the family eventually died out with a Captain John Parr who was buried at Salthouse in 1742. The gallant career of Sir Christopher Myngs was ended by his death from wounds received in action against the Dutch in 1666; and we have Pepys's memorable description of his funeral, at which a party of seamen—"a dozen able, lusty, proper men, with tears in their eyes"—came up to the coach of the high officials of the Navy, and said through their spokesman:

"We are here a dozen of us that have long known and loved, and served our dead commander, Sir Christopher Myngs, and have now done the last office of laying him in the ground. We would be glad we had any other to offer after him, and in revenge of him. All we have is our lives; if you will please to get His Royal Highness to give us a fireship among us all, here is a dozen of us, out of all which choose you one to be commander, and the rest of us, whoever he is, will serve him; and, if possible, do that that shall show our memory of our dead commander, and our revenge."

Sir Christopher's daughter Mary Myngs was buried in Salthouse Church in January 1698, and a stone to her memory is still to be seen there.

The Bredcockes, the Parrs, and a third family, the Stanforths, seem to have been the leading people in Salthouse for several generations. They all owned a certain amount of land, took their turns as churchwardens and in other parochial offices, and had connections with the sea. In 1671 the register records that "Henrie Stanforth, the son of Henrie and Robert the son of Robert Stanforth being drowned at the seashore while trying to save the men of a ship wrecked and aground off [illegible] Sept. 12th were taken up at Cromer and Runton Sept. 15th and buried at Salthouse Churchyard Sept. 18th."

The Stanforths outlasted the Bredcockes and the Parrs, and only came to an end late in the eighteenth century, when their heiress, Margaret Stanforth, married the Rev. Dixon Hoste of Ingoldisthorpe and later of Godwick. Her property at Salthouse was sold; but she transmitted the seafaring traditions of her family and her native village to her son, Sir William Hoste, one of Nelson's most valued captains. Like Nelson, William Hoste was sent to the Paston Grammar School at North Walsham, where one of the houses now bears his name, and went from school to sea in Nelson's own ship at the age of twelve. His friend and contemporary, John Weatherhead, the son of another Norfolk parson, was killed in 1797 in the action at Teneriffe in which Nelson lost his arm. A few weeks afterwards Nelson, referring to the death of Weatherhead in a letter to Hoste's father, added: "Your dear good son is as gallant, and I hope he will long live to honour Norfolk and England"—a hope which Hoste's later career abundantly fulfilled.

LETTING LOOSE THE TAP

"HIS MANAGERS did not keep in due bounds, but let loose the tap all over that large town." So Roger North described the victory of Robert Coke of Holkham in a by-election at King's Lynn in 1675, when he defeated Simon Taylor, a prominent wine-merchant of the borough. At an earlier election, when Roger North's brother Francis was standing, Taylor had himself let loose the tap. He "produced a butt of sherry, which butt of sherry was a potent adversary". Nevertheless North had also prevailed against the local man: and it was not until 1679 that Taylor's ambition was at length fulfilled, and he was able to represent Lynn in the next four Parliaments.

Candidates for Parliament no longer woo our votes with butts of sherry. They no longer open the public houses to all comers, for the duration of the campaign, at their sole expense. They now let loose a different and less costly sort of tap, a torrential flow of promises and assurances. But in the old unregenerate days the electors expected something a good deal more tangible, especially those in the smaller boroughs. They often received it.

Until the Reform Act came into effect in 1832, there were six constituencies in Norfolk—the county, and the boroughs of Norwich, Great Yarmouth, King's Lynn, Thetford and Castle Rising. Each returned two members, so that the thirty or forty electors at Castle Rising had as large a representation in Parliament as the whole great county of Norfolk. The franchise was wildly inconsistent as between one borough and another. Voting for the county was confined to freeholders of land with an annual value of forty shillings and above; so that owners of copyhold land, and men who were tenants but not owners of freehold land, had no votes at all. Even so, the expense of a contested election for the county was so formidable that if the parties could possibly come to a compromise, they always did so. Thus there was no contest for the county seats between 1715 and 1734; then not another until 1768; and then not another until 1802.

But when a contested election did occur, the candidates and their supporters let loose the tap with a will. I have written in *A Norfolk Gallery* of the tremendous elections of 1802 and 1806, when Col. John Wodehouse, the Tory champion, strove to displace Thomas William Coke, the idol of the Whigs. The reckless expenditure of the rival candidates gave rise to the saying "Kimberley oaks against

Holkham purse." The costs of a seventeenth-century election were on a smaller scale; but here also I have lately come upon evidence of the solicitude felt by candidates for the well-being of their voters.

Sir John Hobart of Blickling and William Windham of Felbrigg were the Whig nominees in the second county election of 1679. It was a hurried affair, the outcome of a successful petition which had unseated two Tories. Both sides joined in a frantic rush to hire as many as possible of the Norwich inns, with all their accommodation and all their stores of food and liquor. But in case supplies ran out— and Sir Thomas Browne wrote that he never remembered so great a poll—both candidates hastened to send up further provisions from their estates. "I have ordered the beife to be sent this night to Chapel Field", Hobart wrote to Windham. "Soe likewise I shall what mutton, lamb and other provisions I can possibly gett ready against the time. I wish you would doe the same, for all we can doe within this time will be too little. I wish you could provide lobsters for the better company." In reply Windham undertook to despatch "six peeces of roast beefe, three sheep, three lambs, and lobsters and crabbs".

The boroughs, owing to their divergence of franchise and the different influences which controlled them, present a very varied picture. At Castle Rising, from the late seventeenth century onwards, one seat was controlled by the Howards and the other by the Walpoles. Each family nominated a member, and a feast was jointly given by them to their docile electorate. Thetford was more open to outside influences. Dean Prideaux pronounced in 1708 that "all was sold" in the little borough—"the election there is among the magistracy, and 50 guineas for a vote is their price".

King's Lynn was dominated for many years by the Turners and Walpoles. Efforts were sometimes made to break their hold on the borough, for example by William Folkes in 1747. This was a particularly rowdy election. "The public houses were opened, and continued so", wrote the vicar of the town, "so that here was nothing but men and women and children drunk, old women especially." But Folkes was at the bottom of the poll, and the opposition did not make another attempt until 1768. During part of the interval Horace Walpole joined Sir John Turner in the representation of the borough. He was never opposed; but he did on one occasion take the trouble to go down to Lynn and undergo the ceremonies of an uncontested election. His experiences produced one of the most amusing of all his letters.

"It is plain I never knew for how many trades I was formed, when at this time of day I can begin electioneering, and succeed in my new vocation. Think of me, the subject of a mob, who was scarce ever before in a mob, addressing them in the Town Hall, riding at the head of two thousand people through such a town as Lynn, dining with above two hundred of them, amid bumpers, huzzas, songs, and tobacco, and finishing with country dancing at a ball and sixpenny whisk! I have borne it all cheerfully; nay, have sat hours in *conversation*, the thing upon earth that I hate; have been to hear misses play on the harpsichord, and to see an alderman's copies of Rubens and Carlo Marat. Yet to do the folks justice, they are sensible, and reasonable, and civilised; their very language is polished since I lived among them."

The dinner for the two hundred, of course, was at the expense of his colleague and himself. I am told that the bills for one of his election feasts have lately been discovered. When they are published, we shall see on what scale, and at what cost, the greatest of English letter-writers let loose the tap in his own constituency.

SOME FORGOTTEN PAINTERS

I WISH SOMEONE would compile a biographical dictionary of East Anglian painters. Such a work exists for Devon, and I lately used it with great profit to myself during a visit to that county. Yet even Devon, with its remarkable artistic flowering in the eighteenth and early nineteenth centuries, must yield in that respect to Norfolk and Suffolk. Of course the supreme names—Gainsborough, Constable, Crome and Cotman—have received their due. Their lives have been written, their works carefully recorded. But little information is available, in an easily accessible form, about our excellent painters of the second rank—that most gifted Jacobean amateur Sir Nathaniel Bacon, for example, or Mary Beale, or the delightful Henry Walton. And there are dozens of lesser artists who worked competently and with some reputation in their day, of whom scarcely any biographical details have been assembled.

Take those local portrait-painters whose works are so numerous in the lesser country houses of East Anglia—the father and son

named Heins, Thomas Bardwell, the two Charles Cattons. They produced adequate (though not invariably flattering) likenesses of scores
of ladies and gentlemen who did not care for the trouble or expense
of sitting to a fashionable London artist. And they would occasionally
venture into other fields than portraiture. The younger Heins drew
most of the plates for Bentham's *History of Ely*. Bardwell wrote a
treatise on painting and perspective, explaining the methods by
which he himself had produced copies of the old masters comparable "with any painting that has been done for the past sixty or
seventy years". The elder Catton painted charming landscapes,
sometimes with a suggestion of the early Gainsborough. It would
be agreeable to know more about all these artists than their meagre
entries in the *Dictionary of National Biography* can tell us.

But there are other painters obscurer still, waiting to be "fetched
from the passed world". Perhaps someone in Suffolk knows more
than I do about Robert Cardinall, who in 1725 found it necessary
to insert in the *Suffolk Mercury* a statement that he had studied and
copied for several years under Sir Godfrey Kneller, "notwithstand-
ing which, a certain Envious Person hath declared the contrary to
divers Gentlemen of the said Robert Cardinall's particular acquain-
tance, although the said Person dares not to assert it in the Presence
of the said Robert Cardinall, any more than he dares presume to
paint with him". There are at least two portraits by Cardinall, in the
Duleep Singh collection at Thetford, which certainly show that he
profited from Sir Godfrey's instruction.

Then there was John Davis of Watlington, "a Norfolk gentleman
who has taken to painting", who copied a Dominichino at Houghton
so ably as to arouse the enthusiasm of Horace Walpole. "Do but
figure to yourself," Walpole wrote, "a man of fifty years old, who
was scarce ever out of the county of Norfolk, but when his hounds
led him; who never saw a tolerable picture till those at Houghton
four years ago, who plays and composes as well as he paints, and who
has no more of the Norfolk dialect than a Florentine! He is the most
decent sensible man you ever saw." Walpole gave this copy a place
in his gallery at Strawberry Hill; but although Davis lived until 1778,
I have never heard of any other painting from his brush.

I do not know if it is now possible to identify many works by
Joseph Brown, the Norwich coal-heaver of the mid eighteenth century who taught himself to paint. He first appears in an unpublished
letter of the botanist Benjamin Stillingfleet, written in 1754. "I was
yesterday at Norwich with Marsham where we went to see some

pictures made by a coal-porter who is about 32 or 33 years old. He seems a plain sensible sort of man without any sort of education. He told us he had always had an inclination for painting from his child-hood, and now and then had scrabbled things upon paper, but that he only lately apply'd to it seriously. He has not now actually quitted his first employment, and is very much in doubt what to do, for he gets but little more by his new one, and is not sure of always getting as much in such a tasteless place as Norwich. However as his inclina-tion leads him strongly that way he rather thinks it right to follow it."

Brown's courage seems to have been rewarded. In 1768 Walpole's friend William Cole saw one of his landscapes at the house of a prebendary of Ely. It was "most excellent", he told Walpole; the man must surely be "a great natural genius". And however tasteless Norwich may have been in Stillingfleet's opinion, Brown apparently found employment and consideration there to the end of his days. His portrait—"Joseph Brown, landscape painter, a self-taught artist, and upwards of forty years an inhabitant of this parish"—hangs in the vestry of St Peter Parmentergate, for which church he painted the altar-piece of St Peter and the crowing cock which is now placed above the south doorway.

And while I am on the subject of painting, I would like to men-tion how admirably the full-length portrait of King George III in the Assembly Rooms at Dereham has lately been cleaned. It is a fine example of the official royal portrait which Allan Ramsay painted at the time of the young King's coronation. Copies were turned out in considerable numbers by Ramsay and the assistants in his studio, and were sent as gifts to the crowned heads of Europe, to our embassies and legations abroad, and to many favoured recipients at home. Another example, incidentally, hangs on the great staircase at Blickling Hall. An inscription on the frame states that this copy was presented to the town of Dereham by George, fourth Viscount and later first Marquess Townshend, in 1766. Exactly why Lord Towns-hend made this gift at this particular date, it is difficult to say. Dereham had been regarded in 1750 as "the most Jacobite town in this county"; but by 1766 the Jacobite cause was virtually dead, and there can have been little need to stimulate the loyalty of the people of Dereham towards King George III. Anyhow, there the portrait is, with its blue and gold and ermine once more revealed in all their freshness; and perhaps one lover of painting and history may be allowed to thank the Headboroughs of Dereham—that is their ancient title—for what they have done.

"BATTLES LONG AGO"

IN MY COLLECTION of Norfolk books, a fair-sized shelf is devoted
to the printed matter—it can hardly be dignified with the name of
literature—issued during the Parliamentary elections of the eighteenth and nineteenth centuries. There they stand, pamphlets, poll
books, speeches, collections of squibs and ballads, reports of petitions
and scrutinies; little volumes, most of them, printed in all kinds of
type and encased in every variety of binding. It is curious to reflect
upon the high hopes and bitter disappointments, the careful negotia-
tion and reckless partisanship, the eloquence and anger, the wrangling and uproar, whose last faint echoes still linger in this shelf-full
of tattered books, as I turn their pages in the utter quiet of a country
library on a winter night.

There is every sort of difference between the elections of the
present day and those of earlier centuries. Now, there is universal
adult suffrage; then, the franchise was very limited, and it varied
between a county and a borough, and still more between one
borough and another. Now, the whole nation votes on the same day;
then, the polling at a general election was spread over a much longer
period, and the polling booths in a large constituency remained open
for days and even weeks on end. Now, the ballot is secret; then,
people gave their votes in public, and books were afterwards printed
to show exactly how everybody had voted.

From early times until the passing of the Reform Bill in 1832,
Norfolk returned twelve members to Parliament. The county elected
two members; and two members apiece were returned by each
of the five boroughs—Norwich, Great Yarmouth, King's Lynn,
Thetford and Castle Rising. The two latter were typical "pocket-
boroughs"; they were wholly under the control of neighbouring
grandees, and contained the merest handful of electors, who readily
voted as they were told. I only know of one contested election in the
whole long history of Castle Rising; and that was a by-election in
1673, at a particularly stormy moment in the reign of Charles II.
The candidate nominated by the "proprietor" of the borough was
the diarist Samuel Pepys, who came down to Norfolk anticipating
the usual unopposed return, and was much annoyed to find that
some local Whigs, headed by the Rector of Sandringham, were

accusing him of being a Papist and had put up a rival candidate. However, Pepys was duly returned, by 29 votes to 7.

Voters for the two county seats had to own freehold property of the annual value of forty shillings, which does not sound a very exacting test. But under the manorial system a man might live in great prosperity, possessing a substantial acreage of copyhold land, or paying a very large annual rent as a tenant-farmer, and yet own no freehold property at all; and without that essential qualification he could not claim a vote. In the eighteenth century I doubt if the total number of freeholders in Norfolk ever much exceeded 7000; it gradually rose, however, and early in the next century was approaching 8000. A contested election for the county was a tremendous affair. Every freeholder had to vote in Norwich, whether he lived on the distant coast or in remotest marshland, or in London or even farther afield. It was customary for each candidate to hire a certain number of the inns in Norwich for the accommodation of his supporters. The provision of free food, drink, lodging and stabling for all these voters, together with countless other expenses, made a contested election a costly and sometimes a ruinous business; and in many counties the party leaders always tried to compromise, so that one candidate of each persuasion could be returned and a contest avoided. This was done with great success in Norfolk; during the hundred years after the accession of George I there were only five contested elections for the county seats, in 1715, 1734, 1768, 1802 and 1806. But those were fights indeed—bitter, prolonged, and fearfully expensive to all concerned.

In fiction, the atmosphere of these contests was admirably caught by R. H. Mottram in *The Boroughmonger*—although, to be strictly accurate, the election in that fine novel was for the borough of Norwich, thinly disguised as Easthampton, and not for the county of Norfolk. Every detail of their actual progress, from the nomination of candidates to the triumphal chairing of the victors after the poll had been declared, can be traced in the little books to which I have referred. Most fascinating of all, perhaps, are the printed poll books which tell, parish by parish and hundred by hundred, how the freeholders voted. One can learn from them how small, by modern standards, the electorate was; and how opinion would often be virtually unanimous in one place, and deeply divided in another. In 1806, for example, all but one of the 77 voters in Wells voted the same way, while the 67 voters in Diss and the 72 in East Dereham were almost equally divided. Even as late as 1865, all but one of the

36 electors in Sheringham voted for the same two candidates; and the courageous exception, although his property was in Sheringham, resided safely at Cromer. I can trace in these books exactly how my own forebears, the Cremers of Beeston Regis, voted in every election from 1715, when the printing of votes first began, until 1868, the last General Election before the secret ballot was introduced. Like the great majority of people in the north-east corner of Norfolk, they voted almost consistently for the Whig candidates.

FORGOTTEN CONTROVERSIES

WE LIVE IN AN AGE of many daily newspapers and weekly reviews; and in their pages, with occasional assistance from wireless and television, most of our controversies are thrashed out. They provide the recognised channels for public argument upon matters vital or trivial, national or local, popular or abstruse. But in earlier centuries, and indeed until little more than a hundred years ago, controversies tended to be carried on by means of pamphlets rather than articles or letters in the Press. In those more leisured times a battle of contending pamphlets might rage for months and even for years over any issue upon which people felt strongly or were deeply divided in opinion. And when the battle was over, the pamphlets would often be collected and bound together in a single volume, for future reference and the enlightenment of posterity.

There is a curious fascination about these collections, the repositories of so much forgotten eloquence and argument and indignation. Long-dead voices come to life as one turns the pages, the voices of men and women who were stirred to their depths by some question which the present-day historian will perhaps dismiss in a page or a paragraph. Most old libraries are full of such volumes, covering an extremely wide range of topics. From them one can learn every possible argument for and against such once burning issues as stage licensing, and the reform of the calendar, and the new-fangled notion of inoculation against smallpox, and the game laws, and the corn laws, and the regrettable "enthusiasm" of the Methodists, and the alarming doctrines of Tom Paine.

Here is a volume of seventeenth-century political wranglings in which the leading combatant is Roger L'Estrange, the most active and vociferous controversialist whom Norfolk has yet produced. Close by are some productions by his only possible rival for that distinction, Richard Gardiner, who made such a nuisance of himself in our local affairs in the reign of George III. Here are volumes of conflicting arguments about the courts-martial of Admiral Byng and Lord George Sackville, the great naval and military *causes célèbres* of the eighteenth century. Next to them stands a collection of pamphlets about the death of Sir Robert Walpole, in which his own doctors explain why he died, and several other doctors maintained that he would still be alive if they had been in charge of him. In another shelf are volumes devoted to the great impostures of the eighteenth century, each which produced its crop of pamphlets— the poems attributed to Ossian, and Rowley the priest of Bristol; Elizabeth Canning, who was supposed to have been kidnapped and starved by a gipsy; Mary Tofts, whose claim to have given birth to a litter of rabbits was the subject of long and heated debate in the medical profession.

The first decades of the nineteenth century, with their urgent religious and political issues, tended to be fruitful in controversy. I do not know whether this was especially so in Norfolk; but I have lately acquired certain volumes of pamphlets which show that many eager pens were then at work in this part of the country, particularly in the ranks of the clergy. At that period Thomas William Coke of Holkham, the leader of the Whig interest, was the most influential figure in Norfolk, and had represented the county in Parliament for many years, although the Tories had lately succeeded in capturing the second seat. Bishop Bathurst of Norwich was also an ardent Whig, and at one time the solitary supporter of his party upon the episcopal bench. There was a close alliance between the Whig potentate and the Whig prelate; and in spite of their personal regard for their Bishop, certain of the Tory clergy of the diocese could not always let his public utterances pass without remonstrance. A strong and sometimes irrelevant political undercurrent is often noticeable in the local pamphlets of the day, whether they deal with the tithe system, or the poor law, or missionary societies, or the dangerous encroachments of Popery.

The leading champion on the Whig side was the redoubtable Archdeacon George Glover, Rector of Southrepps and Vicar of Cromer, an assiduous and hard-hitting pamphleteer. Before me lie two of his rejoinders to the Rev. Robert Forby, Rector of Fincham, who had ventured to address a pamphlet to the Bishop. "It has always been my practice through life", the Archdeacon begins, "to listen with as much patience to those who differ from my opinions as the imperfections of my nature will allow": after which he lays into the author of the *Vocabulary of East Anglia* with the most obvious enjoyment. In the same volume he is himself assailed, over one of his own pamphlets on the subject of tithe, by the Rev. William Tilney Spurdens, Curate of Crostwight with Honing and Chaplain to the Earl of Stradbroke, another important figure in East Anglian philology. But he really met his match in the Rev. George Burges, Vicar of Halvergate and Moulton, who must surely have been the most militant of all these Tory clergymen. Mr Burges nicknamed Glover "the Cardinal of Cromer", called him "a Holkham political hack", and asserted, probably with truth, that he could "get you up an election daub at twenty minutes' notice".

I long to find out more about Mr Burges, that gallant and incorrigible Tory fanatic. His principal work, published in 1819, runs to no fewer than 362 pages of breathless denunciation of the Whigs in general, of Mr Coke and Archdeacon Glover in particular, and of "that overwhelming democratical spirit which is ready to seize and raven upon us all". Later pamphlets from his pen are in the same strain. Even in 1835 the Whigs were about to "shiver to atoms the corner stones of our constitution in Church and State, and lay our cathedrals and our palaces in the dust". He died in 1853, in his nine-tieth year; and probably, in that high Victorian noon, he was still expecting presently to hear the tumbrils of the English Revolution.

WOLTERTON HALL

This essay was written in January 1953, a few weeks after the fire at Wolterton. The hopes expressed as to the restoration of the house have been splendidly fulfilled.

IN 1727 THE POLITICIAN AND DIPLOMATIST Horatio Walpole, younger brother of the Prime Minister, Sir Robert Walpole, began to build his fine new house at Wolterton, and in 1741 he was able to record its completion on a tablet above the east doorway. The architect was Thomas Ripley, who was also largely responsible for Sir Robert's great mansion at Houghton and for the Admiralty building in Whitehall. Everyone has admired Wolterton, with its dignified proportions and the subtle contrasts of its red brick and grey Portland stone, from that day to this; even Horatio Walpole's extremely critical nephew, Horace Walpole of Strawberry Hill, pronounced that it was one of the best houses of its size in England. Successive generations of the family filled it with works of art of every kind—paintings, tapestries, furniture, statuary, porcelain and glass, a noble library of books. On the fifth of December 1952 fire broke out in an upstairs room. By nightfall the upper floor and the roof had been burnt, the second floor severely damaged, and the lower rooms, with all their superb plasterwork and other decoration, flooded deep in water.

There is something profoundly depressing, an air of utter futility and waste, about the aftermath of a fire. The other day I explored the upper floors of Wolterton Hall—a wilderness of charred beams, blackened plaster, gaping windows, and huge tarpaulins flapping dismally where the roof had been. It was indescribably sad, and hardly less so in the state rooms beneath, where the great Prime Minister had discussed the affairs of Europe with his brother, and Nelson had come to dine on his return from sea, and Cotman had admired the paintings, and now the splendid cornices and mouldings were blotched and stained by the torrents of water. Yet the situation might well be far worse. The damage to the two lower floors is not irreparable; thanks to the skill and exertion of the firemen, the estate staff, and indeed the whole neighbourhood, the treasures of the house were saved almost without exception; and, most important of all, the owners are quietly determined, in the face of every discouraging circumstance, that Wolterton shall be restored as soon as possible to its former amenity and beauty.

During the past few summers the principal rooms at Wolterton have been opened to the public every week. Hundreds and perhaps thousands of visitors have admired the paintings and tapestries which covered the walls, now so discoloured and bare. There are exciting stories of how some of these lovely things were rescued only just in time, with the flames roaring overhead. Even the great conversation-piece by Amiconi, showing Horatio Walpole with his wife and their numerous children, was removed to safety. In the nineteenth century this remarkable group had been divided into five pieces, which were framed and hung as separate pictures. A few years ago the present Lord Walpole had it put together and restored to its original condition; and the work was done so skilfully that not the smallest trace of its dismemberment was visible. It was rehung in its former position in the dining-room on the first floor. At the height of the fire the estate foreman, Mr Newstead, with great presence of mind had one of the windows removed with its entire frame; and the enormous picture was lowered through the space and reached the ground almost undamaged.

Another celebrated picture at Wolterton is the pastel of Horace Walpole in masquerade dress, done by Rosalba Carriera at Venice in 1741. He once wrote to a friend, "You know I can't resist going to a fire, for it is certainly the only horrid sight that is fine"; and on another occasion, "I am as constant at a fire as George Selwyn at an execution." He described several London conflagrations with great vividness in his letters; and it would have intrigued him vastly to know that during the fire at Wolterton his portrait was one of the first to be carried to safety, and that it now gazes down from the place of honour in the temporary quarters which Lord and Lady Walpole will occupy during the rebuilding of their home.

As the result of modern fire-fighting technique and skill, and the magnificent solidity of eighteenth-century building, and the efforts of so many willing helpers, Wolterton and its contents have survived. The pictures will one day hang once more on the walls, and the damaged plasterwork will be renewed. The books, in their handsome bindings of calf and vellum and morocco, will return to the shelves which now stand empty and forlorn. Visitors will once again admire the tapestries given to Horatio Walpole by Cardinal Fleury in remembrance of their private friendship and their public association, which for many years so greatly benefited both England and France. Nelson's bust will resume its place, and Richardson's portrait of Pope, and the huge Nankin bowl in which generations of Walpoles are said to have been christened. The fire of 1952 will be nothing but an agonising memory.

These noble Palladian houses, secluded in the depths of our countryside, are a part of English history and of the English achievement. Their architecture and decoration, pictures and furniture, gardens and parks form a precious legacy from the greatest century of European civilisation. And despite the difficulties of the present age their story is not yet concluded, their usefulness is not yet past. Norfolk may well be grateful to everyone who helped to save Wolterton and its treasures, and above all to its indomitable owners.

INDEX

Adams, Sir Thomas, 102
Addison, Rev. Leonard, 65–6
Anne, Queen, 57–8, 60
Ashly, Robert, 41
Ashwellthorpe, 11
Astley, Herbert, Dean of Norwich, 51
Attleborough, 61
Aubrey, John, 98
Audley, Hugh, 26
Aylsham, 16, 17, 61

Bacon, Sir Edmund, 60–2
Bacon, Sir Nathaniel, 109
Bacon, Sir Nicholas, 99
Bacon, Nicholas, 15
Bacon, Robert, 18
Baconsthorpe Castle, 33, 89–92
Baker, Rev. Thomas, 65–6
Bardwell, Thomas, 110
Barningham, Little, 27
Barningham, North, 17
Bathurst, Henry, Bishop of Norwich, 115
Bawburgh, 66
Bawdeswell, 98
Bayfield, 25
Beale, Mary, 109
Bedingfeld family, 38
Beeston Regis, 114
Bendish, Mrs (née Bridget Ireton), 38–9
Bixley, 34
Blennerhassett family, 55–7
Blennerhassett, John, 55–7
Blickling, 28, 80, 84, 99

Blomefield, Rev. Francis, 57, 61, 68, 79, 91, 101
Bowman, Rev. Thomas, 65–7
Bradfer-Lawrence, H. L., 47
Brampton, 50
Bredcocke family, 105–6
Bredon, Rev. William, 92
Brigstowe, William, 96
Brokett, Rev. John, 40
Brooksbank, John, 40
Brown, Joseph, 110–11
Browne, Sir Thomas, 13, 15, 29, 32, 46, 49–52, 56, 96, 100–1, 108
Browning, Robert, 11, 12
Brundall, 61
Bulwer, Roger, 18
Burges, Francis, 57
Burges, Rev. George, 116
Burton, William, 34
Buxton, John, 34–5

Caister-on-Sea, 55–7
Calthorpe, Sir Christopher, 42–4
Calthorpe, James, 42
Camden, William, 98
Cardinall, Robert, 110
Castle Rising, 19, 34, 60, 107–8, 112–13
Catton, 61, 85
Catton, Charles, 110
Cawston, 65–7
Charles I, King, 19–21, 24, 29, 47, 91, 102

Charles II, King, 42, 44, 47, 95, 99, 102, 103

Chaucer, Geoffrey, 98

Cholmondeley, Marquess of, 40

Church, Barnard, 34

Clarendon, Edward Hyde, Earl of, 34–5

Claypole, Elizabeth (*née* Cromwell), 37

Cock, Charles George, 34

Coke, Sir Edward, Chief Justice, 99

Coke, Robert, 61–2, 107

Coke, Thomas William, afterwards 1st Earl of Leicester, 99, 107, 115–16

Cole, Rev. William, 111

Collinges, Rev. John, 46

Cooper, Rev. Thomas, 27

Corbet, Clement, Chancellor of Norwich, 14

Corbet, Miles, 38

Corbet, Richard, Bishop of Norwich, 14

Costessey, 61

Cotman, John Sell, 79–81, 109, 117

Cremer family, 114

Cremer, Rev. Thomas, 40

Crome, John, 109

Cromer, 16, 61, 68–70, 80, 114, 115

Cromwell, Henry, 37

Cromwell, Oliver, 28, 34–9

Cromwell, Richard, 37

Cross-grove, Henry, 57–9, 61

Curll, Edmund, 49–50

Davis, John, 110

Desborough, Major-General John, 34

Diss, 61, 113

Docking, 61

Downham Market, 27

D'Oyley, Sir William, 35–6, 45

Eachard, Rev. Laurence, 23

Earsham, 23

East Barsham, 42

East Dereham, 25, 27–8, 61, 84, 111, 113

Easton, 25, 27

Edgefield, 27

Elizabeth I, Queen, 31, 91, 99

Evelyn, John, 13, 34

Fairfax, Henry, Dean of Norwich, 55

Faithorne, William, 42

Fakenham, 27, 42–4, 61

Felbrigg, 32–3, 80, 92, 102

Fersfield, 61

Fincham, 77

Fitch, Robert, 93

Fleetwood, Mojor-General Charles, 35, 38

Folkes, William, 108

Forby, Rev. Robert, 77–9, 115–16

Frenze, 55

Frere, Tobias, 35

Fuller, Rev. Thomas, 13, 14, 94, 98, 104

Garboldisham, 60

Gardiner, Richard, 115

George I, King, 57, 113

George III, King, 111, 115

Gill, Rev. Thomas, 68

Gillingham, 15

Gleane, Sir Peter, 46–9

Gleane, Sir Thomas, 47

Glover, Archdeacon George, 115–16

Gooch, Sir Thomas, Bishop of Norwich, 101

Great Yarmouth, 16, 29–31, 34, 38, 60, 63–4, 107
Grigor, James, 84–6
Grimston, 39–41
Guestwick, 18
Gunton, 60

Hall, Joseph, Bishop of Norwich, 29, 50, 100
Hampden, John, 37
Hanworth, 80
Harbord, William, 60
Hardwick, 46–7
Hare, Sir Ralph, 35–6
Heigham, 61
Heins, D., 110
Hellesdon, 61
Hengrave, 14
Heveningham, William, 38
Hevingham, 16–18, 84
Heydon, 17
Heydon family, 33, 89–93
Heydon, Sir Christopher (i), 89, 91
Heydon, Sir Christopher (ii), 90, 92
Heydon, Sir Henry, 89
Heydon, Sir John (i), 90
Heydon, Sir John (ii), 90, 91, 92
Heydon, Sir William, 90
Heydon, Lady (*née* Mirabel Rivett), 92–3
Hindolveston, 31
Hingham, 61
Hobart, Edmund, 28–9
Hobart, Sir Henry, 99
Hobart, James, 27–8
Hobart, Sir James, 51
Hobart, John, 35–6
Hobart, Sir John, 28, 35–7, 45, 108
Hobart, William, 27–8
Holkham, 61, 84, 102, 107

Holt, 17, 25, 27–8, 61
Horningtoft, 77
Horsford, 61
Hoste, Rev. Dixon, 106
Hoste, Admiral William, 106
Houghton, Mr, 20–1
Houghton Hall, 40, 117
Hudibras, 18, 22, 50

Inglott, William, 51–2
Intwood, 28
Ireton, Bridget (*née* Cromwell), 38–9
Ireton, Henry, 38–9
Itteringham, 80
Ives, John, 62–4
Ivory, Thomas, 69

James I, King, 95, 99
James II, King, 42
Jay, Christopher, 30–1
Jenkins, John, 103–4
Jermy, Col. Robert, 25–7
Jewson, C. B., 66

Kemp, Sir Robert, 45
Ketteringham, 38
Key, John, 11, 12, 96
Keynes, Sir Geoffrey, 49–50
Kimberley, 61, 103, 107
King's Lynn, 27, 34, 38, 60, 102, 105, 107–9
Kitson, S. D., 79, 80
Kneller, Sir Godfrey, 110
Knevet, Rev. Ralph, 15–16, 96–7
Knyvett, Sir Thomas, 11–13
Kytson, Sir Thomas, 14

Lambert family, 94
Lenthall, William, 26
L'Estrange family, 94
L'Estrange, Sir Nicholas, 43
L'Estrange, Roger, 115
Letheringsett, 18

Lightbody, John, 71–3
Lindsey, Mathew, 28
Lloyd, William, Bishop of Norwich, 43
Love, Barry, 63

Manchester, Edward Montagu, Earl of, 22–3
Mannington, 17
Marsham, Robert, 16, 111
Martham, 65–7
Martin, Thomas, 92
Mattishall, 25
Mingay, John, 101
Morden, William (afterwards Harbord), 60–1
Mottram, R. H., 70, 113
Myngs, Sir Christopher, 105–6
Myngs, Mary, 106

Nelson, Rev. Edward, 61
Nelson, Horatio, Viscount, 61, 106, 117–18
Ninham, Henry, 84–5
Norden, John, 98
North, Roger, 103–4, 107
North Walsham, 11–13, 95, 97, 106
Norwich, Bishops of (see under Corbet, Wren, Hall, Sparrow, Lloyd, Trimnell, Gooch, Bathurst)
Norwich Cathedral, 16, 29–31, 50–2, 55, 96, 100–2
Norwich, churches in,
  St Giles, 59
  St Gregory, 103
  St Peter Mancroft, 47, 99
  St Peter Parmentergate, 111
Norwich, cult of flowers at, 13–15
Norwich, early newspapers in, 57–9, 81–3
Norwich, politics in, 16, 29, 45, 57, 70–2, 82–3

Old Buckenham, 26, 61
Oxborough, 61
Oxnead, 15, 49, 50, 89, 93–7, 102

Paine, Sir Joseph, 103
Paine, Thomas, 114
Palgrave, Sir Augustine, 100
Palgrave, Sir John, 17
Parkin, Rev. Charles, 61
Parr family, 105–6
Parsley, Osbert, 52
Paston family, 38, 93–7
Paston, Clement, 93–6
Paston, Sir Edmund, 11
Paston, Lady Katherine (*née* Bertie), 94–6
Paston, Lady (*née* Katherine Knyvett), 11
Paston, Margery, 93–4
Paston, Robert, 1st Earl of Yarmouth, 42, 45–6, 47–9, 94–5
Paston, Sir William (1479–1554), 93
Paston, Sir William (1528–1610), 11–13, 95–7
Paston, Sir William (1610–63), 15, 18, 94
Paston Grammar School, 11–13, 95, 97, 106
Pepys, Samuel, 100, 105, 112–13
Playters, Sir John, 24
Playters, Rev. Sir Lionel, 21–4
Pockthorpe, 55–6
Porter, Rev. Edmund, 16
Postwick, 61
Potts, Sir John, 17–18, 20–1
Pride's Purge, 24
Prideaux, Humphrey, Dean of Norwich, 43, 101, 108
Proctor, Rev. William, 23

Ramsay, Allan, 111
Rant, Sir Thomas, 102
Repton, Humphry, 85, 90
Rhodon and Iris, 15–16, 96
Ripley, Thomas, 117
Rowe, John, 56

Sall, 19–20
Salthouse, 104–6
Sancroft, William, Archbishop of Canterbury, 45
Sandringham, 112–13
Saxlingham, 89, 90, 92
Sheringham, 61, 80, 114
Skippon, Major-General Philip, 34
Sotherton, Thomas, 35–6
Sotterley, 21
Sparrow, Anthony, Bishop of Norwich, 44–6
Spelman, Sir Henry, 19
Spelman, Henry, 104
Spelman, Sir John, 19–21
Spelman, John, 19
Sprowston, 61, 102
Spurdens, Rev. W. T., 78, 116
Stanforth family, 105–6
Stanton, William, 55
Stiffkey, 99
Stillingfleet, Benjamin, 69, 111
Stoke Ferry, 77
Stone, Nicholas, 94–6, 102
Stratton Strawless, 84
Strode, William, 14–15
Sufferings of the Clergy (John Walker), 21–4
Swaffham, 27, 61
Symonds, Nathaniel, 63

Taylor, Simon, 107
Taylor, William, 83
Thetford, 27, 34, 60, 107, 110, 112
Thorowgood, Rev. Thomas, 40–1

Thorpe, 85
Thorpe Market, 85, 102
Thorpland, 42
Thurloe, John, 37
Tibenham, 34
Tilles, Rev. Michael, 13
Tillett, Jacob Henry, 82
Tittleshall, 102
Took, Mr, 71–3
Townshend, Charles, 2nd Viscount, 99
Townshend, Hon. Charles, 99
Townshend, George, 1st Marquess, 99, 111
Townshend, Sir Horatio (afterwards 1st Viscount), 33, 35–6, 44–5
Trimnell, William, Bishop of Norwich, 101
Turner, Dawson, 77, 79–81
Turner, Rev. George, 77
Turner, Sir John, 108
Tuttington, 80

Uggeshall, 21–4

Walpole, Horace, 4th Earl of Orford, 63, 108–9, 110–11, 117–18
Walpole, Horatio, 1st Lord Walpole of Wolterton, 99, 116–18
Walpole, Sir Robert, 1st Earl of Orford, 60–2, 99, 115, 116–17
Walpole, Robert, 7th Lord Walpole of Wolterton, 117–18
Walsingham, 17, 27
Walton, Henry, 109
Walton, Col. Valentine, 38
Ward, Edward, 34
Watlington, 110
Waxham, 47–9

Wearing, S. J., 95
Weatherhead, John, 106
Wells, 61, 113
Wickmere, 80
Wilby, 34
William III, King, 42–3
Wilton, Robert, 34–5
Windham, Judge Francis, 99
Windham, John, 32–3, 91
Windham, William (1647–89), 44–5, 108
Windham, William (1717–61), 69
Windhamt R, Hon. William (1750–1810), 99
Winey, Andrew, 41
Winfarthing, 84
Wodehouse, Sir Armine, 61

Wodehouse, Col. John, 107
Wodehouse, Sir Philip, 35–6
Wodehouse, William, 60–2
Wolterton, 20–1, 80, 85, 116–18
Wren, Matthew, Bishop of Norwich, 23
Wrench, Sir Benjamin, 61
Wright, William, 11, 12
Wycherley, William, 99
Wymondham, 84
Wyndham, John, 69
Wyndham, Thomas, 68–9

Yarmouth (see Great Yarmouth)
Yarmouth, Earls of (see under Paston)